TEACHER RESOURCE BOOK
Foundation-2

SPELLING RULES!

Second edition

Tanya Gibb

macmillan education

This edition published in 2016 by

macmillan education

MACMILLAN EDUCATION AUSTRALIA PTY LTD
15–19 Claremont Street, South Yarra 3141
Visit our website at www.macmillaneducation.com.au
Associated companies and representatives throughout the world.

Publisher: First edition Sharon Dalgleish
Designers: Trish Hayes and Stephen Michael King
Illustrator: Stephen Michael King

Printed and bound in the UK by CLOC Ltd.
MEA9_2019

Dictionaries to support the ***Spelling Rules!*** program

Ages 6–10

Ages 10–15

Contents

Introduction

Spelling Rules! is a bestselling series of seven student books and two Teacher Resource Books, which have been reproduced in a second edition. This second edition includes a disc in the Teacher Resource Books, Scope and Sequence charts updated for the Australian Curriculum and reflection activities in student books 1–4 to allow students to assess their own progress.

The *Spelling Rules!* program is based on sound learning theory and pedagogy, using strategies that embed spelling in the long-term memory. The program systematically develops phonological, visual, kinaesthetic, morphemic and etymological spelling knowledge so that students learn *how* to spell at the same time as they are learning the spelling of specific words.

The *Spelling Rules!* student books and Teacher Resource Books work together as a complete spelling program. They can also be used independently as stand-alone resources for student use or teacher reference.

The *Spelling Rules!* program has been designed to provide spelling instruction that is systematic, purposeful and sequential. Each student book includes a scope and sequence chart and units of work for students to complete. Each unit focuses on one or more English language sounds or letter patterns. These sounds or letter patterns are featured in the word list for each unit.

High frequency words are also included in the word lists. High frequency words are words that students are likely to encounter when reading, and that they are likely to need when expressing their own ideas in writing. It is useful for students to learn the spelling of high frequency words because automatic spelling recall helps increase their fluency when writing.

Activities in the student books focus specifically on the words in the word lists and also on teaching spelling in the context of reading and writing. Many activities incorporate vocabulary development and understanding of grammatical patterns to assist students in creating their own effective written texts.

It is recommended that students spend a small amount of time practising their spelling each day. Focusing on a few words at a time, and reinforcing these, has proven to be the best way to ensure students retain spelling knowledge. It is anticipated that each unit in the student books will be completed over the course of a school week, with the extra activities suggested in the Teacher Resource Book used to supplement and reinforce all aspects of the student books.

Learning to Spell

Why Do We Need to Learn to Spell?

Spelling is a tool for writing, in making meaning, in communicating effectively and to assist in 'getting the message across' to the reader. Writers need to spell consistently and according to the conventions of the language they are writing in so that their writing can be read by others. It is also useful as a reader to have an understanding of spelling, to help make sense of a written text, although you do not need to be a good speller to be a good reader.

Why Is It Hard to Learn How to Spell?

Spelling is a highly complex process. It involves selecting the correct pattern of letters to represent the sounds in speech. In English writing, this means learning 26 letters of the alphabet and combining them to represent approximately 40 speech sounds or phonemes – and there are over 600 combinations of letters to use to represent those 40 phonemes. No wonder spelling can be difficult! And no wonder it is important to explicitly teach students the system.

Another aspect of English that has rendered its spelling more challenging is the fact that English has adopted many words from other languages, and the spelling of these adopted words usually reflects the spelling – but not always the pronunciation – of the original language. *Yacht* is an example. Understanding that this word was adopted from the Dutch *jacht* can help students understand why the spelling does not reflect the English pronunciation.

Also, pronunciations have changed over time so that the spelling of some words no longer reflects their pronunciation. *Knew* and *gnaw* are examples: originally the *k* and the *g* were pronounced, and the spelling remains the same even though the pronunciation has changed.

Homophones also add to the complexity of spelling in English. Homophones are words that sound the same but have different spellings and meanings, for example *there, their* and *they're*.

For some learners of English as a second language, there are certain sounds that are difficult to hear or difficult to pronounce. For example, for speakers of Spanish as a first language, /th/ in *them* can easily become /d/; Arabic speakers might have difficulty distinguishing between /p/ and /b/; and Japanese speakers might have difficulty distinguishing between /l/ and /r/.

It's important to stay aware of the special circumstances of all your students and be prepared to remedy any difficulties.

How Do Students Learn to Spell?

It is likely that you will encounter a minority of students who are natural spellers. These students will become quite proficient spellers without explicit teaching instruction. However, even these students will stumble over spelling an unknown word unless they have been given the knowledge to help them work out how to go about it.

Students need to be taught how to spell. Providing them with books and writing opportunities is a part of the equation, but these strategies will not, in themselves, teach the majority of students to spell. The vast majority of students need formal, systematic and sequential instruction. They need to be taught how spelling works, as well as the strategies and knowledge they can use to become independent, confident spellers and spelling risk-takers.

To make progress as spellers, students need opportunities to engage in writing every day. The more time students spend engaged in writing activities, the more opportunities they have to try out what they are learning.

Types of Spelling Knowledge

Learning to spell involves the following types of spelling knowledge:

Phonological knowledge uses memory of how a word sounds, and of the patterns of sounds in words. It relates to students' aural skills.

Visual knowledge uses memory of how letters and words look, and of the visual patterns in words. It relates to students' visual skills.

Kinaesthetic knowledge uses the physical memory of the feeling when saying different sounds and words, and when writing the shapes of letters and words. It relates to tactile perceptual awareness.

Morphemic knowledge involves an understanding of the meaning or function of words, or parts of words, and applying this knowledge to spelling. It involves thinking skills.

Etymological knowledge involves an understanding of the origins and history of words and the effect these have on spelling patterns. Remembering and making analogies involves thinking skills.

Making Spelling Stick

According to current brain research theory, the brain and its functions can be likened to a computer. A computer's hard drive can be compared to our long-term memory. That's where we store information that we want to be able to retrieve at any time in the future for re-use. The human brain has a huge capacity for long-term storage.

The RAM or useful working memory of a computer is finite. If we overload a computer or expect too much of it at any one time, it will freeze or send the message 'not enough memory'. The working memory in a human brain is also finite. Students need opportunities to process new information and then store it in their long-term memories (internal hard drive) for future use. It helps students to be exposed to small amounts of new information at a time. To expect them to learn too much at one session is asking for that 'not enough memory' message.

Another useful computer analogy is that if we work on a computer but don't save the files, they disappear. If new information in the brain's working memory is not transferred to long-term memory, it will be lost. If we want student brains to recognise that spelling retention is important, then we need to present small amounts of spelling to them at any one time, and then give them time to reinforce, practise and consolidate this information so that it is saved in their long-term memories. Otherwise, their brains will do the equivalent of sending it all to the trash. Human brains sort out the trash from the useful knowledge that's worth storing while we are asleep. This is why, as teachers, we sometimes feel that we are getting nowhere, having to re-teach the same information for weeks, with none of it seeming to sink into students' brains. Repeated exposure to information in small doses and plenty of practice will ensure that the information (spelling knowledge) gets saved in students' long-term memories.

Our brains also establish links and pathways between old information and new information. A sequential spelling program that builds on previous learning makes learning to spell a more manageable task for students. Presenting information to be learned through auditory, kinaesthetic and visual experiences supports students' differing learning styles, and multiple sensory experiences also assist in establishing these connections and building on knowledge.

The *Spelling Rules!* program is designed to ensure that students commit spelling knowledge to long-term memory. An acronym that can summarise the strategies that will help spelling move from working memory to long-term memory is **SLLURP**.

Say the word carefully and slowly to yourself.
Listen to how each part of the word sounds in sequence.
Look at the patterns of letters in the word and the shape of the word.
Understand rules, word meanings and word origins.
Remember similar words you can already spell and relate this knowledge to any new word.
Practise writing the word until it is firmly fixed in long-term memory. A useful sequence for students to use is **'look, say, cover, write, check'**.

Spelling Stages

There are **five** stages of spelling that students progress through, at individual rates, in order to become successful spellers.

Student Books Foundation, 1 and 2 in this series focus on the first three stages, which are the **pre-phonetic** stage, the **early phonetic** stage and the **phonetic** stage.

The five spelling stages are linear but at times a student may be operating in two stages at once. For example, a competent speller who usually operates in the conventional stage might become a phonetic speller when attempting to spell a word that is totally unfamiliar such as a mathematical or scientific term.

The Pre-Phonetic Stage

The pre-phonetic stage is when students first become aware of print. They might ask you to write a shopping list for them, or notice when you skip words in a story that they have heard before. They understand what print is for, but they do not yet understand how it works.

The student might use invented letters as well as some copied and conventional letters and/or scribble. They will 'read' it aloud to you, because they understand the concept that writing can be read and that the message remains constant.

Supporting the Learner

- Ensure that students can hear individual words in a stream of speech by speaking slowly and clearly. When you read big books or class books, point out in the text where each word ends and the next word begins.
- Explore with students the sounds in words. Show how words can be separated into individual sounds and how the sounds can then be rejoined.
- Write *with* students, *in front of* students and *for* students as their scribe. Encourage students to write, scribble and experiment.
- Teach the conventions of English print. Show students how print in English is read from left to right, a page is read from top to bottom, and a book from front to back.

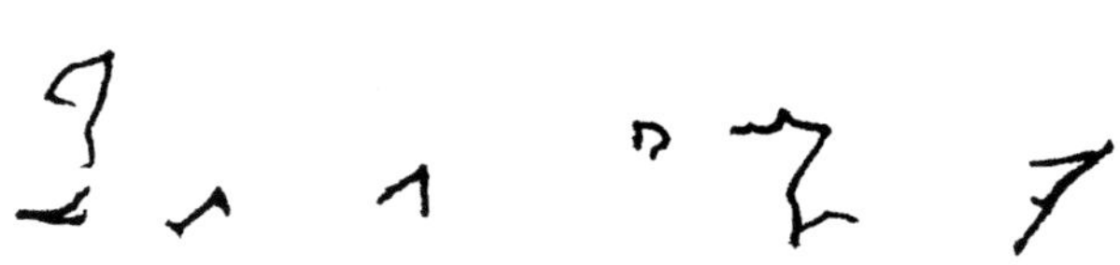

The child is becoming aware of print conventions and is drawing scribbles and pretend letters. This needs to be interpreted and 'read' by the child. The sample 'reads': *Dear Aunty Helen.*

The Early Phonetic Stage

In the early phonetic stage, students are starting to associate sounds with symbols and might recognise some letters in the environment, for example on shop signs or in their name.

They might use consonants or single letters to represent words or sounds in their writing. They are developing their knowledge of letters. Students are starting to understand sound–letter relationships and to spell words with two letters, or words with three letters that follow the pattern consonant–vowel–consonant (CVC) such as 'mum'. They might also have started to develop a list of high frequency words that they recognise from their reading and use in their writing, including their own name or the names of siblings or friends.

Supporting the Learner

- Reinforce students' early understanding of sound–letter relationships, especially through using CVC patterns (mum, dad).
- Sound out words with students.
- Clap out the syllables in words or make up actions for the syllables in each child's name. For example, 'Waiyin' could have two jumps.
- Ask students to listen for initial and final sounds in words.
- Provide lots of opportunities for students to engage in writing and encourage students to 'have a go' at spelling.

The student understands that writing is meant to be read and that the message can be read consistently. The student is not able to recognise individual words in a stream of speech and therefore omits the gaps between words when writing. The student writes all the letters known in upper-case except for 'li', which forms part of her own name, 'Ali'.

The student relies on memory to 'read' the text *This is Ali's work.*

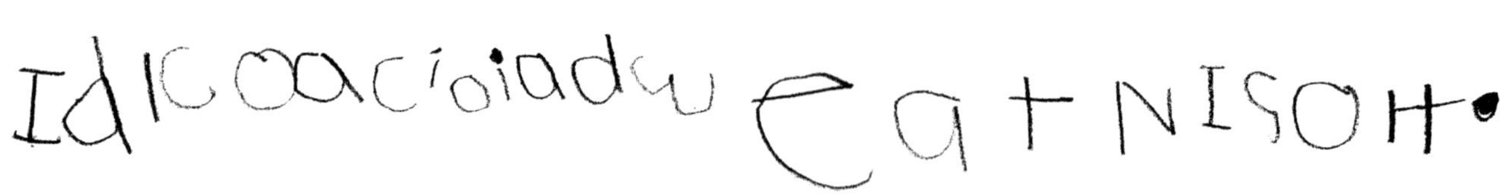

The student is associating symbols with sounds. The student has started the sentence string using an upper-case I and completed it with a full stop. The writing still contains a mixture of upper-case and lower-case letters.

The sentence reads: *I did cooking and we ate it.*

The Phonetic Stage

In the phonetic stage, students represent words in a phonetic way. Their writing can often be read quite well by adults because it is logical and students show an understanding that they need to match letters for sounds.

Students are starting to show awareness of spelling rules and some conventions of written language such as full stops.

A vocabulary of high frequency words is being stored in the long-term memory and students are able to retrieve these words when required.

Supporting the Learner

- Explicitly teach letter–sound correspondences and provide opportunities for students to practise their newly acquired knowledge.
- Help students remember spelling patterns by explicitly examining words that include the patterns and pointing out significant visual features as well as mnemonic clues.
- Teach students how to examine the visual patterns and shapes of words.
- Point out examples in student writing or class reading where sounds need combinations of letters to represent them, for example '*sh*op'.
- Support students in developing a core vocabulary of high frequency words and ensure you help them store the words in long-term memory.
- Begin to teach students about prefixes and suffixes as required in their writing.
- Teach students about word families.
- Teach students about contractions, for example *I'm, don't.*
- Explicitly teach students strategies for working out the spelling of unfamiliar words. Articulate for them the strategies you would use. Say to students, 'Let's sound it out . . . Let's write it and see if it looks right . . . Let's think about other words that sound the same – do we know how they are spelt?' And so on. Thinking out loud like this as a model for students helps to reinforce what they can do when spelling an unfamiliar word.
- Have students write specific texts such as letters, cards, shopping lists, stories and poems.
- Introduce proofreading strategies.
- Play spelling games or games derived from spelling practice, for example Scrabble®, bingo, snap.

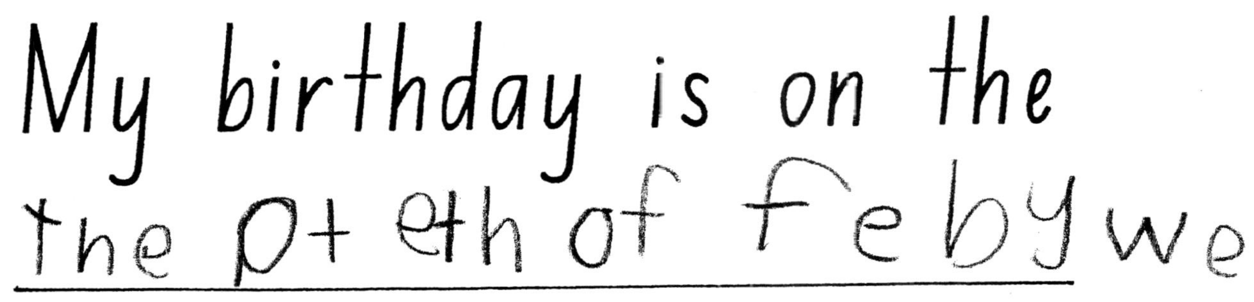
My birthday is on the
the 0th eth of febywe

High frequency words are correct (*the* and *of*). It is possible to read the student's writing and the student is starting to form words — *febywe* is a phonetic attempt to spell *February*. (It is also possible the student is not pronouncing *February* in a way that will assist even phonetic spelling attempts.) The text reads: *the 9th of February*.

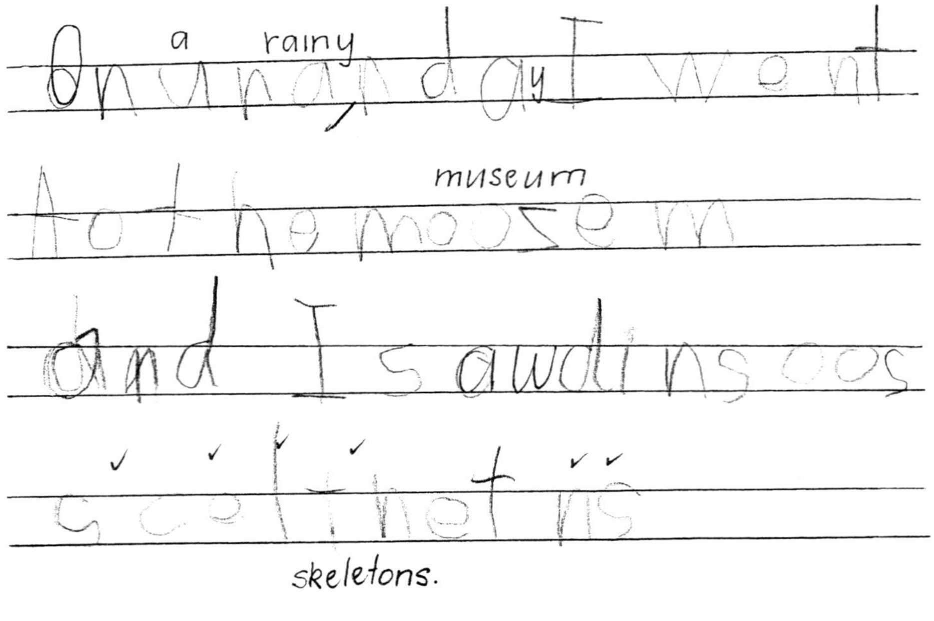

The student's writing is progressing, but is still phonetic. Words are seen as discrete units and are written separately. High frequency words are usually written correctly (*on, I, to, the*). There is the correct use of upper-case *I*, and the self-corrected use of upper-case to start the sentence. Less common words are spelt phonetically using some letters to represent many (*sceltnetns* for *skeletons*). The student is prepared to tackle quite complex vocabulary. Correct pronunciation and sounding out the word might have assisted the student when attempting to spell *museum* (*moozem*) and *dinosaurs'* (*dinsoos*).

The sentence reads: *On a rainy day I went to the museum and I saw dinosaurs' skeletons.*

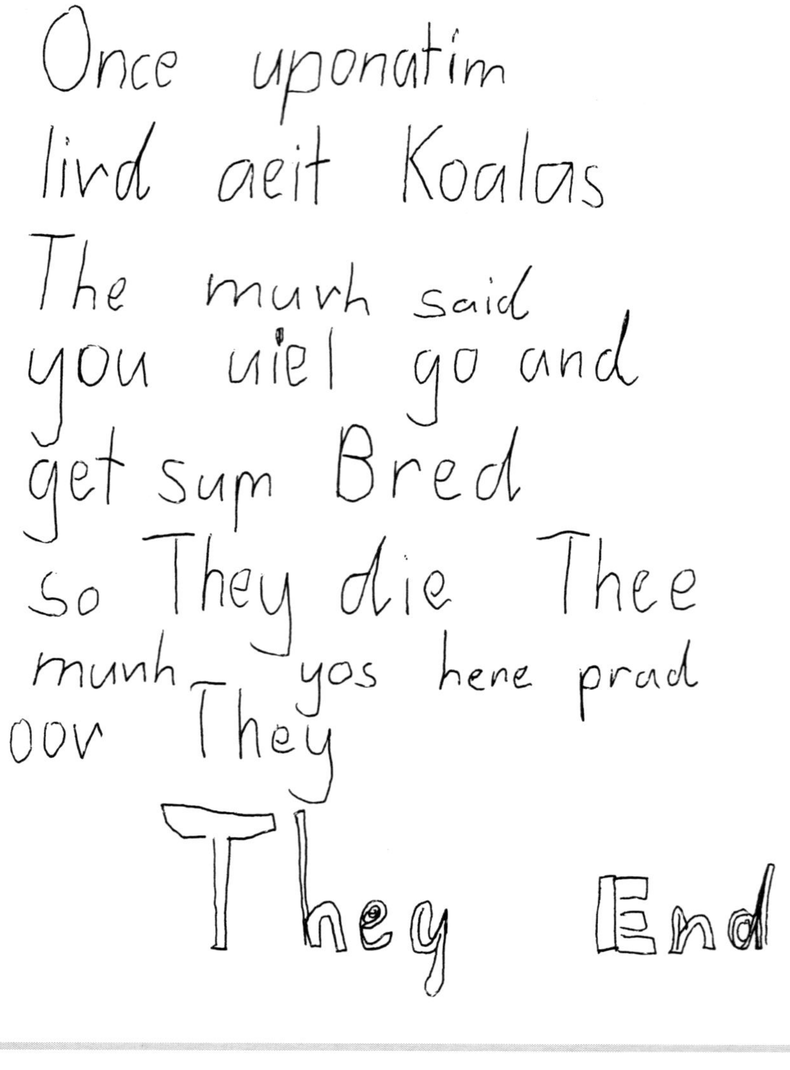

The text is relatively easy to read and all words are written as discrete units. The student is spelling some high frequency words correctly (*and, the, they, you, said*), but not others (*die* for *did*, *oov* for *of*). The student is still approaching spelling phonetically, but the phonetic spelling is not completely regular. The student copied *Once upon a time* from the board, but did not correctly copy *time*. The student is not pronouncing *mother* correctly, and has misspelt it twice using *muvh*. The student is adding extra letters because he or she is stretching the words to sound them out, hence *uiel* for *will*.

The text reads: *Once upon a time lived eight koalas. The mother said you will go and get some bread so they did. The mother was very proud of them.*

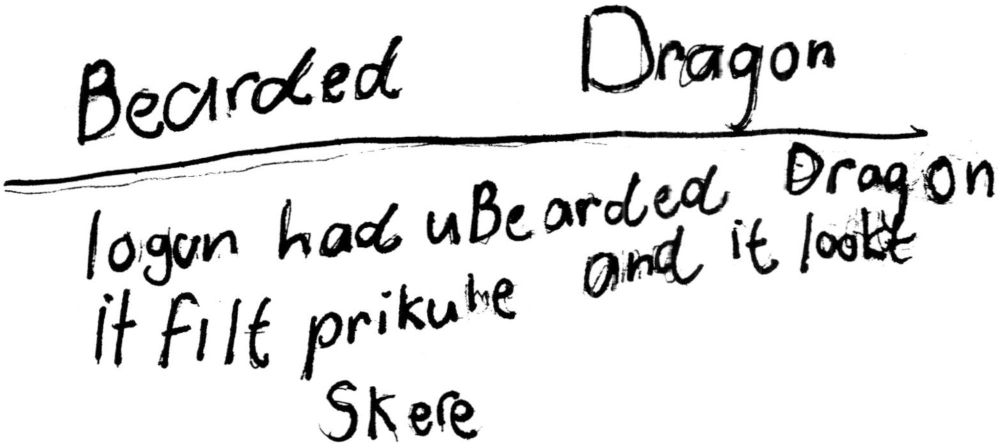

The student is spelling high frequency words correctly (*and, it, had*), but is still approaching spelling phonetically. The text is easy to read: all words are written as discrete units and the phonetic spelling is fairly regular. The student has correctly copied *Bearded Dragon* from the board. The student does not use *y* for the short *y* sound at the end of the word *prickly (prikule)*. The student is not pronouncing *prickly* correctly, having stretched the word to sound it out, and has added an extra vowel sound between *k* and *l*. The student has not learned the suffix *ed* for *looked (lookt)*. The student is not pronouncing *felt* correctly, and has spelt it *filt*. The student does not recognise a sentence.

The text reads: *Logan had a bearded dragon. It felt prickly and it looked scary.*

The Transitional Stage

In the transitional stage, students become aware of factors other than phonics that they can bring to spelling, for example visual knowledge of the way words look; knowledge of particular spelling patterns, especially more common ones such as *ing, ed, scr, ay*; knowledge of spelling rules such as 'change *y* to *i* before adding *-ly*'; and understanding of word families. They are able to use syllabification and morphemic knowledge.

They are able to use analogy to work out how to spell words or parts of words. They might know how to spell *day* and *fry* and so spell *Friday* as *Fryday*.

Students have developed a substantial core vocabulary of high frequency and subject-specific words.

Supporting the Learner

- Explicitly teach spelling patterns to students.
- Build on student understanding of word families.
- Extend students' understanding of the use of morphemes and etymology to remember spelling patterns.
- Encourage students to use visual knowledge to check spelling.
- Further develop students' list of high frequency words.
- Encourage students to write, and ensure they have a variety of purposes for which to write.
- Encourage students to read, and ensure they are exposed to a variety of texts.
- Expect that students will proofread their own work.

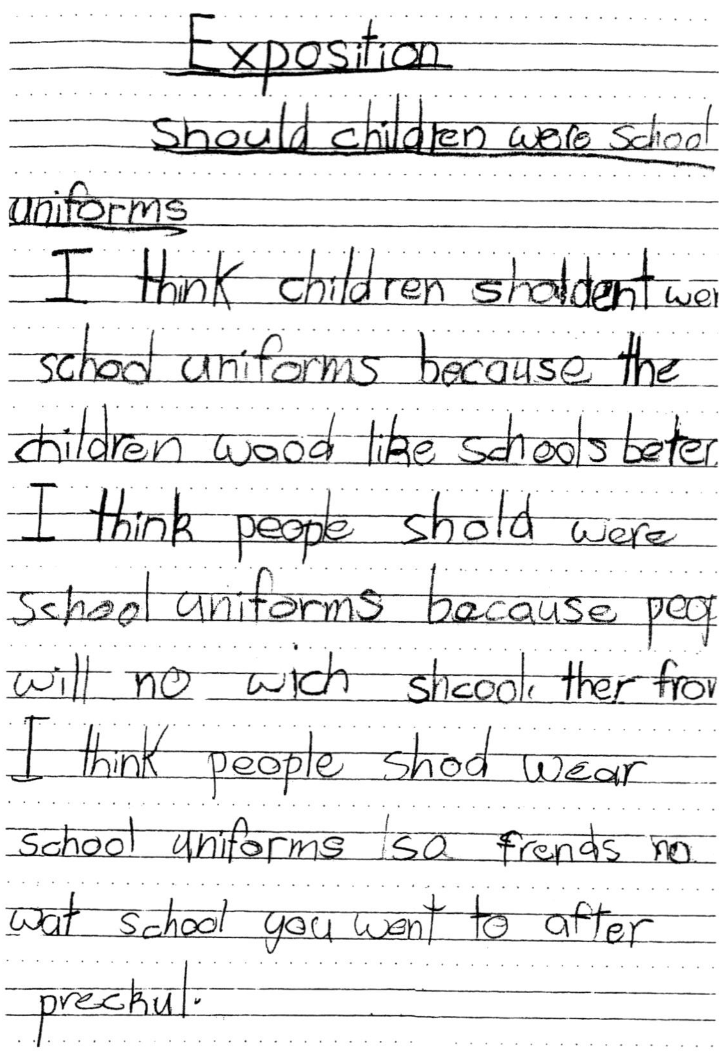

Exposition
Should children were school
uniforms
I think children sholdent wer
school uniforms because the
children wood like schools beter.
I think peope shold were
school uniforms because peq
will no wich shcool ther frov
I think people shod wear
school uniforms so frends no
wat school you went to after
preckul.

The student has committed to memory some high frequency words with common letter patterns: *think, because, so, went.* Errors are still made: *frends.* Words are spelt in different ways within the same piece of writing: *shold* and *shod* for *should; school* and *shcool* for *school* and *preckul* for *preschool*; and *were* and *wear* for *wear.* The more common word of a homophone pair has been used: *wood* for *would* and *no* for *know.*

The text is easy to read.

The Conventional Stage

In the conventional stage, the speller knows the rules and conventions of English and understands the complex relationship between sound and letter representation. Students will often know when they cannot spell a word. Conventional spellers use a variety of strategies to work out how to spell unfamiliar words and to remember known words, including the use of external references such as dictionaries. They have a large number of learned words, including subject-specific vocabulary, that they can retrieve from their long-term memory.

Supporting the Learner

- Support students as they further develop their use of phonological, visual, kinaesthetic, etymological and morphemic knowledge to spell. For example, *phonological*: revise irregular or uncommon letter patterns; *visual*: ensure that students are exposed to and focus on visual patterns in words; *kinaesthetic*: writing and typing words for themselves to support physical memory of the shapes of letter patterns and words; *etymological and morphemic*: thinking about word origins, word families and connections between words supports the brain in storing spelling in long-term memory.
- Expect students to have a comprehensive list of words that they are able to retrieve from their long-term memory to use in their writing.
- Ensure that students are given opportunities to read and write more complex texts for a range of purposes.
- Expect that students will proofread their written work with a high degree of accuracy, using external references when necessary.

Last Thursday we had a swimming carnival. I went in a breast stroke race but I didn't go in any others. I got lots of Lollies for cheering.

High frequency words are correctly spelt. The student is applying rules (for example, doubling the *m* in *swim* when adding *-ing*). The student has correctly used the upper-case for *Thursday* and an apostrophe to indicate an abbreviation in *didn't*.

Glossary of Spelling Terms

Affix
The general term for a prefix or suffix, i.e. a morpheme added to either the beginning or end of a base word.

Analogy
Equivalence or likeness. Recognising how to spell one word because of its similarity to another, e.g. *sip* and *pip*.

Antonym
A word or word group with a meaning opposite to that of another word or word group, e.g. *full* and *empty*.

Auditory perception
Ability to distinguish sounds.

Base word
The basic form of a word, e.g. *help*. Prefixes and suffixes are added to the base word to change the meaning, indicate tense, form the plural etc., e.g. *helped, helping, helpful* etc.

Blend
A combination of two consonants in which each retains its distinctive sound, e.g. /br/ in *bread*, /cl/ in *clasp*.

Compound word
Two or more words joined together to produce a new word with a different meaning, e.g. *wheel + chair* → *wheelchair*.

Consonant
All the letters of the alphabet that aren't vowels.

Contractions
Formed when two words are combined and then a letter or letters are omitted, e.g. *didn't* for *did not*, *I'll* for *I will*. Apostrophes are used in place of the deleted letter or letters.

Conventional speller
Someone who understands the conventions of spelling and applies them consistently when spelling.

Digraph
A pair of letters that represent a single speech sound, e.g. *ea* in *beat*, *sh* in *shop*, *ar* in *dark*.

Early phonetic speller
Someone who is starting to associate sounds with symbols and might recognise some letters in print.

Etymology
The origin and history of a word. It can often assist in understanding the reason for a word's spelling.

Final sound
The last sound heard in a word, e.g. /d/ in *bread*

Grapheme
The smallest unit of writing to represent a sound, e.g. *t* in *tip*, *th* in *these*, *mb* in *thumb*.

High frequency words
Words that are commonly used in texts and speech.

Homographs
Words of different origin and meaning that are spelt the same, e.g. *live* in *I live at home* and *a live one*; *bear* in *polar bear* and *to bear a burden*.

Homophones
Words that are pronounced the same but have different spellings and meanings, e.g. *deer* and *dear*.

Initial sound
The first sound heard in a word, e.g. /s/ *in stop*.

Invented spelling
Spelling made up when a child is first learning to write. Sometimes called *temporary spelling*.

Letter–sound relationship
The way a sound is represented in writing.

Long-term memory
Where information is stored for later retrieval.

Medial sound
A sound that occurs within a word or syllable that is neither initial nor final.

Minimal pairs
Two words that differ by only one phoneme, e.g. *hot/hat, get/pet*.

Mnemonic
A memory cue, e.g. The *princi<u>pal</u> of a school is my <u>pal</u>.*

Morpheme
The smallest grammatical unit of language that has meaning. It can be a word, e.g. *sit* or *by*, or an element of a word, like *mis-* in *mistake* or *-ing* in *singing*.

Morphology
The study of word formation in a language by analysing word parts and word derivation.

Onset and rime
The beginning part or sound of the word is the onset and the rest of the word is the rime, e.g. *m–atch*. The breaking of words into beginnings and endings.

Peer assessment
Assessment undertaken by peers.

Phoneme
The smallest unit of sound in a language.

Phonemic awareness
Ability to recognise that words are made up of individual sounds (phonemes) and use letter–sound correspondences to read and spell words. (Sometimes used interchangeably with *phonological awareness*.)

Phonetic speller
A speller who represents words in a phonetic way.

Phonological awareness
Ability to recognise larger units of sound in addition to phonemes, e.g. syllables, onset and rime. Enables students to recognise and generate rhyming words, count syllables, and separate the beginning and ending of words. (Sometimes used interchangeably with *phonemic awareness*.)

Phonology
The sound system of language.

Prefix
An affix attached to the beginning of a base word to change the meaning, e.g. the prefix *un-* + base word *like* → *unlike*.

Pre-phonetic speller
A speller who is just becoming aware of print. They might use invented letters as well as some copied and conventional letters and/or scribble.

Pronunciation
The act of producing speech sounds.

Proofreading
Checking a written text for correct spelling and other conventions of writing such as punctuation and grammar.

Root word
See *Base word*.

Sight word
A common word that often cannot be sounded out and that needs to be memorised, e.g. *the, said, come*.

Silent letter
A letter that does not represent a sound, e.g. *w* in *wrestle*, *k* in *knight*, *l* in *folk*.

Suffix
An affix attached to the end of a base word to change the meaning, e.g. the suffix *-ly* + base word *like* → *likely*.

Syllable
A unit of sound within a word, e.g. *to-mor-row*. A syllable must contain a vowel or the letter *y* when it is acting as a vowel. Syllables usually start with a consonant: *Sa-tur-day*. Double consonants are usually split down the middle: *hap-py*. A word consisting of one syllable is *monosyllabic*. A word consisting of two or more syllables is *multisyllabic* or *polysyllabic*.

Synonyms
Words that have the same or similar meaning, e.g. *throw* and *toss*.

Tense
The form of the verb that shows time. Auxiliary verbs and/or suffixes attached to the end of the base form of the verb are used to show when an action happens, e.g. *She plays. She is playing.* (both are present tense) *She played.* (past tense) *She will play.* (future tense)

Transitional speller
A speller who is starting to use knowledge of particular spelling patterns, spelling rules, word families, syllabification and morphemes as well as phonological knowledge to spell words.

Upper-case and lower-case letters
Two forms of the letters of the alphabet. Upper-case letters are used to indicate the beginning of a sentence or the initial letter of a proper noun.

Visual perception
Ability to distinguish between shapes, objects and patterns by using the sense of sight.

Vowels
The letters *a, e, i, o* and *u*. The letter *y* is a semi-vowel, as it is a consonant that sometimes represents a vowel sound.

Developing a Whole-School Spelling Policy

A consistent approach to the teaching and learning of spelling throughout the school will benefit students, their families and staff. An important first step in implementing a whole-school approach to spelling is to develop a spelling policy.

How to Develop a Whole-School Spelling Policy

To begin with, staff members or a small subcommittee of staff members can meet to discuss how spelling is currently taught, what the school community (including families) expects regarding the teaching and assessing of spelling, what expectations there are of student achievement, and how government testing results and government benchmarks affect spelling in the school.

A written survey for all staff members or by grades or year groups will elicit the sort of information required by the Spelling Committee. Ask questions such as: How do you currently teach spelling? Are you confident that the approach you use is working? For all students? For the majority of students? Which students are not benefiting from the school's current approach to spelling? What is best about the school's current approach? What concerns do you have about spelling in your classroom and across the school? What would you like to see happen regarding spelling across the whole school? What support would you like in order to implement a whole-school approach?

Schools might also find it useful to gain the support of families at this stage. If a whole-school approach is to be implemented then the support of families in policy input and purchasing of resources, as classroom volunteers and at-home spelling partners, will be necessary as well as appreciated. The Spelling Committee could devise a questionnaire for families so that the views of parents and caregivers are taken into account when formulating the school's spelling policy.

What Constitutes a Whole-School Policy?

On pages 17–19 you'll find a sample policy to use as a starting point. Adapt it to suit your school's needs. It contains the following sections:

Philosophical Statement and Rationale
Why is a whole-school program needed? What does the school value and believe about spelling? What particular learners is the school made up of (e.g. Indigenous, ESL, students with special needs)?

Aim/s Clearly articulate the overall aim/s of a whole-school approach to spelling.

Objectives Make broad statements of the values and attitudes, skills and knowledge that are promoted by the school's policy.

Curriculum Links or Standards These can be found in the Australian Curriculum and will be available in each state's syllabus document.

Student Assessment Outline the ways of collecting, recording and using assessment information in the school.

Teaching Implications Cover the time frame for policy implementation (including factors such as the funding and purchasing of resources, teacher in-service training, training requirements of volunteers, staff meetings, team meetings and so forth) as well as:

- how spelling will be taught in each year group and to the range of learners in the school, including the possibility of subject-accelerated progression in the area of spelling for gifted spellers
- how and when students will be assessed and how the assessment information will be reported to families
- the role of families in supporting the development of their child's spelling as well as each student's role and responsibilities.

Support Material/Resources Which resources will be used/purchased? Who will be responsible? Will the school purchase a commercially available whole-school program such as *Spelling Rules!*?

Evaluation How will the policy be evaluated and revised, by whom and in what time frame?

Scholarsville School

Whole-School Spelling Policy

Philosophy

The staff and families at Scholarsville School believe that learning how to spell correctly is a valuable tool for reading and writing and as such is useful across the entire school curriculum.

We recognise that:

- not all students will be natural spellers and that some students will struggle to attain and retain spelling knowledge
- learning to spell is a complex task involving phonological, visual, kinaesthetic, morphemic and etymological knowledge and that individual students will rely to a different extent on each area of spelling knowledge
- the vast majority of students need formal, systematic and sequential instruction about the way spelling works, as well as the strategies they can use and the knowledge they can develop to become independent, confident spellers and spelling risk-takers
- all students need support in spelling, including struggling spellers, gifted spellers, students for whom English is a second language, and Aboriginal and Torres Strait Islander students
- the working memory of a human brain is finite. Students need to be exposed to small amounts of new spelling information at any one time. They then need opportunities to practise and consolidate this new information so that it is stored in their long-term memories for future use.

Rationale

The enrolment at Scholarsville School includes 35% of students who are from non-English-speaking backgrounds. These students, as well as our students with English home language backgrounds, need a coherent, systematic teaching approach to spelling so that they develop the knowledge and skills to support effective written communication in English.

Aim

The aim of the whole-school spelling policy is to provide all students with systematic and sequential instruction in English spelling so that they develop positive attitudes to spelling, learn strategies to support their spelling learning and experience success in spelling.

Objectives

1. Students will value correct spelling and develop confidence in themselves as learners of spelling.
2. Students will develop phonological, visual, kinaesthetic, morphemic and etymological spelling knowledge.
3. Students will develop skills and strategies to help them remember spelling and tackle new words.

Curriculum Links

See Australian Curriculum, English.

In their Foundation year of schooling, students will:

- develop positive attitudes about spelling and attempting to spell
- recognise the different sounds in English and isolate sounds (phonemes) in words
- name all lower- and upper-case letters and recognise the most common sound represented by each letter
- recognise rhyme, alliteration, onset and rime, and syllables, and use these to spell words
- recognise and write some high frequency words
- learn to spell consonant-vowel-consonant (CVC) patterns using short vowel sounds, moving on to CCVC (like *ship*) and CVCC words (like *hill*), still using short vowel sounds
- begin to develop the skill of proofreading for correct spelling.

In Year 1, students will:

- build on the skills and knowledge developed in the first year of schooling
- make new words by adding, deleting or substituting letters
- spell single-syllable words with short vowels, common long vowels, some consonant blends and consonant digraphs
- understand how a letter can represent more than one sound
- spell some two-syllable words
- learn how to use mnemonics and analogy to attempt to spell new words
- develop further understanding of word families and rhyming words
- recognise and write some high frequency words
- learn some spelling rules
- begin to learn how to proofread
- develop an understanding of alphabetical order and dictionary use.

In Year 2, students will:

- build on the letter patterns introduced in the first two years of schooling by learning about other digraphs and blends, irregular plurals, and silent letters
- understand that a sound can be represented by different combinations of letters
- read and write an expanding range of high frequency words
- learn to use a variety of strategies to work out spelling: visual knowledge, morphemic and etymological knowledge, analogy, mnemonics
- learn some spelling rules and conventions
- learn about prefixes, suffixes, verb tense and contractions, and develop an understanding of how words are built upon a base word/how word families are formed
- explore and build compound words.

In Year 3, students will:

- build on the skills and knowledge learned in the previous years of schooling with emphasis on the use of etymological knowledge, suffixes, prefixes, homophones, medial double consonants, apostrophes, capitalisation and spelling rules; write more complex texts for varying purposes and audiences; and develop an expanded vocabulary.

In Year 4, students will:

- build on the skills and knowledge learned in the previous years of schooling, with emphasis on spelling strategies needed to tackle unknown words, common prefixes and suffixes, word endings (such as *f*, *ff*, *ph* and *gh*), words adopted by English from other languages, abbreviations, more complex spelling rules, homophones, proofreading and subject-specific words.

In Year 5, students will:

- build on the skills and knowledge learned in the previous years of schooling; learn more about synonyms and antonyms; explore etymology, especially words with Latin, French and Greek roots; learn about acronyms, blends and eponyms; and explore subject-specific words.

In Year 6, students will:

- build on the skills and knowledge learned in the previous years of schooling, as well as reviewing all spelling rules and conventions; conduct a more detailed etymological and morphological study of words; review all affixes, words with difficult or irregular spelling patterns, homophones and homographs; explore subject-specific words; and use proofreading as an automatic process.

Student Assessment

Student spelling achievement will be assessed weekly in each class, by class teachers, using a combination of students' writing samples, dictation tests and tests of the spelling lists covered in the *Spelling Rules!* program.

Information about students' spelling achievement will be recorded and this information will be provided to families informally, as the need arises, and formally, in response to requests from families or as determined by the teacher.

Families will be provided with half-yearly and yearly written reports that outline spelling progress and development.

Teaching Implications

The school will implement this policy commencing Term 1.

Each class will spend 15 minutes per day on explicit spelling instruction. Spelling instruction will also be integrated across all areas of learning. Spelling instruction will be supported by the classroom expectation that all students will engage in writing, daily, for a variety of purposes and audiences, and that this writing will be context based.

Spelling instruction will be part of each day's program as well as occurring spontaneously during the course of any activity that provides a teaching opportunity for spelling.

Support Material/Resources

Spelling Rules! resources will be purchased for each student and class teacher during Term 4 of the year before use. Teachers will familiarise themselves with the program.

In preparation for implementation of this policy, year-group meetings will be held on the first Mondays in October, November and December.

Whole-staff training and professional development opportunities in spelling will be organised.

Evaluation

Evaluation of the policy and policy review will commence in October. Year-group meetings will be held on the first Mondays in October, November and December. Year groups will provide written feedback to the Spelling Committee about the impact of this policy on students and staff.

The Spelling Committee will compile a written report for the school community on the progress of policy implementation, and make further recommendations to school management regarding teacher training, resources (personnel and equipment) and so on.

Scholarsville School

How to Set Up the Classroom for Spelling

A spelling classroom for Foundation to Year 2 will feature a selection of texts on display or readily accessible to students and equipment for experimenting with words and spelling. This equipment might be part of a spelling learning centre, established in one area of the classroom. It is also important that classroom management practices support students' acquisition of spelling knowledge.

TEXTS ON DISPLAY OR READILY ACCESSIBLE TO STUDENTS

These can include:

- lists of useful words: names of students, topic words, high frequency words, word families, days of the week, months, a weather chart with words to attach for *hot*, *windy*, *cloudy*, *rainy* and so on
- lists of stories read, poems learned, songs known
- a class timetable
- class rules constructed with student input: *Walk inside, Use inside voices, Look after property, Put things away, Listen to your friends*
- signs and labels on all items and art work, constructed with student input, e.g. *art cupboard, teacher's desk, Goldie the Goldfish*
- examples of student texts
- student stories and other texts that have been handwritten by you or another adult, or published on a computer
- class books created jointly with the students (and opportunities for these to be borrowed by students to share with their families at home)
- attractively presented and interesting reading materials, both literary and factual
- dictionaries, word books, student spelling books, personal word lists, 'have a go' books.

A SPELLING LEARNING CENTRE

Establish a spelling learning centre in your classroom for interested students, students who need extra spelling practice, or able spellers wanting more challenges. Games and activities could be for individual students, or students could be allowed to work in pairs or groups. The spelling centre could also be used when parent helpers and volunteers are available (or 'buddies' from older classes, if your school supports this practice).

The spelling learning centre could include equipment such as:

- task cards in a box, with word searches, tongue twister challenges, crossword puzzles
- spelling games – Scrabble®, Boggle®, bingo, teacher-created games and resources
- assorted writing materials: whiteboards, paper, cardboard, marker pens, felt pens, pencils, chalk, charcoal, crayons
- magnet letters, letter tiles, letter cards, alphabet charts
- play dough for making letters, and to improve hand strength and therefore fine motor control
- a sand trough for writing words and letter shapes
- magazines, scissors and glue
- computers and tablets
- audio recordings of poems, stories, chants and recorded sounds
- percussion instruments to repeat sequences of sounds or rhythm patterns, or to create beats for the syllables in words.

Classroom Management Practices that Support Spelling Development

To support spelling development:

- allow time for students to write and spell every day
- encourage reference to written language in the classroom during the week, and allow time to revisit and re-read the written texts and to point out aspects of spelling
- provide specific lists of spelling words for students to learn. These lists need to be based on letter patterns or sounds and provide a clear scope and sequence of spelling skills. The lists should also allow for the addition of high frequency words and words from students' own writing
- encourage students to refer to a wall chart that lists steps they can follow in working out how to spell a word, for example **Reproducible 1**, blown up to A3 size
- include parents and other volunteers, and/or peer tutors
- use varied grouping arrangements (ability grouping, mixed-ability grouping, pairs, small groups, mixed-age groups).

Developing Auditory, Visual and Kinaesthetic Perception

It is important to develop auditory, visual and kinaesthetic perception in young children, because these form the basis for the development of phonological, visual and kinaesthetic spelling knowledge, among other things.

Auditory Perception

Auditory perception can be developed using the following activities:

- recognising and labelling sounds
- repeating a sequence of sounds
- learning to distinguish beginning, final and middle sounds in words
- breaking a word into component sounds or syllables
- clapping out a rhythm
- clapping the syllables in words
- recognising rhyming words, alliteration and assonance, onset and rime
- using 'look, say, cover, write, check'.

You will find that during early spelling development students will more readily hear the sound at the beginning of a word. They are usually next able to identify the final sound, and then lastly the sounds in the middle of a word.

Visual Perception

Visual perception can be developed using the following activities:

- learning to really look at letters, and combinations of letters
- distinguishing between letters in written activities (e.g. by colouring every *t*)
- looking at the shapes and lengths of words (e.g. the different shapes of *dog, elephant*)
- using consistent letter shapes and neat writing so that letters and words are easily recognisable
- taking a mental picture of a word, and writing it in the air with eyes closed
- using 'look, say, cover, write, check'
- doing any activity that requires students to use their eyes to problem-solve: jigsaw puzzles, categorising words by shape, matching and sorting words into word families, sequencing objects by colour, shape, size.

Kinaesthetic Perception

Writing is the most important strategy in developing kinaesthetic perception. The act of physically forming the letters with the hand allows the body to store the memory in the same way that learning the position of the letters on the keyboard allows people to type automatically and fluently, without thinking about where the letters are. The hand and brain remember how to write high frequency words without the brain consciously needing to think about it.

Other strategies to develop kinaesthetic perception are:

- writing letter combinations and words using a variety of implements (paintbrushes, crayons, charcoal, collage) and on paper of differing colours and sizes; making letters in sand trays or with play dough, mud, bread dough, biscuit dough
- clapping the syllables in words
- using 'look, trace, cover, write, check'
- using correct pencil grip – because of its importance to hand comfort and writing fluency. Ensure that students hold their writing implements in a grip that will support ease of movement and good visibility.

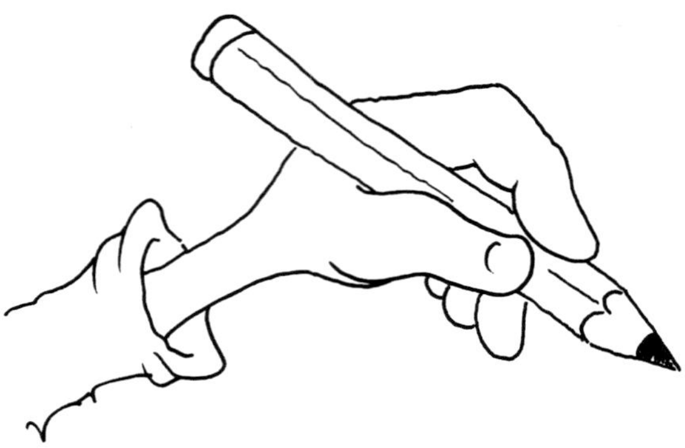

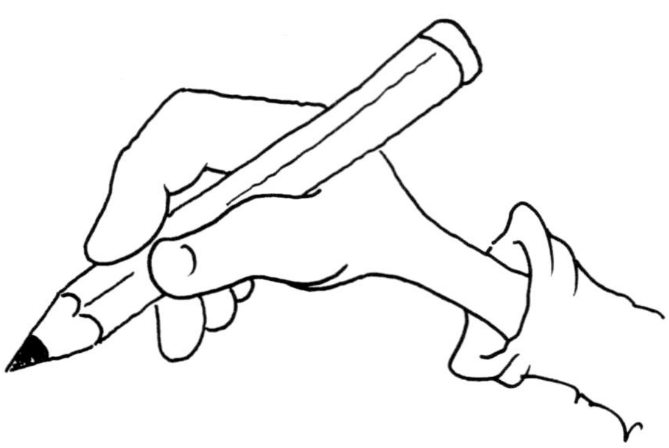

Integrating Spelling into the Reading and Writing Program

There are many opportunities to integrate or connect spelling into the reading and writing program as a whole.

Modelled Writing and Joint Construction

Write texts in front of students, and demonstrate for students how you think as you write. Encourage students to contribute to the text, and discuss and incorporate their ideas and suggestions.

Write books as a whole-class or focus group activity. Books can be based on any topic, and can include photos and factual information related to another learning area; for example, a book could be based on a class excursion or a visit by a guest speaker, or modelled on a picture book the class is reading.

Proofreading

Proofreading is an important part of the writing cycle and should not be confused with the editing process. Editing is when students read over their work to ensure that it communicates what they mean. When students edit their work, they look at aspects such as the structure and grammar of the text and the vocabulary they have used to convey their meaning.

When students are proofreading they are ensuring that their writing is ready for publication. Students need to understand that clear written communication requires correct spelling, punctuation and grammar.

Proofreading skills will develop according to the age and stage of development of students. Before students start proofreading, they need to know what they should be looking for, and how to make the corrections. Remind students that the aim of proofreading is to find any mistakes. Students can use reference materials and refer to their friends as well as referring to you to help them work out what corrections they need to make.

Students are more likely to spot an error in unfamiliar work, so encourage students to proofread each other's writing. Taking a break before returning to a text will help students to spot their own errors.

Impromptu Spelling Conferences

When a student asks for help to spell a specific word, you could take the time to hold a mini-conference with the student. For example, you can point out the spelling features of the word and focus the student's attention on ways to remember how to spell that word in the future. The word can also be added to the student's personal spelling book. Some of these spelling patterns might be useful to teach to the whole class, and they can be the basis for generating extra class word lists or word banks.

Personal Spelling Books or Word Books

All students should have a personal spelling book or word book in which they record their personal spelling lists and the high frequency words that they are using as well as the words they are encountering in their spelling program. They could also record spelling rules, conventions and spelling tips. Students should be encouraged to keep these personal spelling books from year to year, and to refer to the books when they need to check the spelling of a word that they have attempted to spell before.

It is also useful to have a section of the personal spelling book devoted to parent and teacher communication. You can report on students' spelling development, and parents can inform you about progress at home regarding spelling.

A good early word book to use is *My Macquarie Word Book*, which has been designed specifically for Australian students. It is arranged alphabetically and supports the learning of letter names. It also reinforces the fact that spelling is important for all subjects, and is not relevant only to English.

Dictionaries and Reference Materials

Dictionaries and spellchecker computer programs are useful tools in helping students spell words they want to use. Students need support when they first start using reference materials, or they can become discouraged, unable to work out how to look up a word in the dictionary or how to choose the correct word from the alternatives offered by the computer spellchecker program.

It is important to introduce students to an age-appropriate dictionary when they are starting to read and learning to spell. Initial activities should include looking up words to find out their meanings, and working out that a word's meaning depends on how it is spelt.

Students also need to be taught that dictionaries contain more information than the meaning of words and their correct spellings. As students' word skills develop, they can focus on the origin of the word, and the word family to which it belongs. Morphemic and etymological knowledge support students in spelling words that cannot be tackled phonetically.

Plan activities that will assist students in exploring the contents of dictionaries. For example, choose a different page of the dictionary for each student. Ask each student to select the word on their page that they think is the most interesting/easy to spell/difficult to spell. Ask each student, in turn, to write their word on the board and then explain why they selected it.

Have a selection of dictionaries and other reference books available, and encourage students to refer to these resources. *The Macmillan Australian Primary Dictionary* (for students aged from six to ten years) supports the *Spelling Rules!* program.

If students are using spellcheckers or other electronic devices, teach them how and when to use them. Explain to students that while computer spellcheckers are useful, they will not pick up correctly spelt words that are misused. Students will still need to proofread their work. An over-reliance on spellcheckers early in a student's spelling development could lead to poor proofreading skills. Students can miss finding errors in meaning and context when a word is chosen for spelling correctness only (for example, 'Stir the *flower* into the cake mix'). All this needs to be carefully explained to students. It is more likely that a computer spellchecker program will be taught after Year 1.

Word Research

Word research activities involve students in finding out the origins or history of words. They could start with local words such as the names of suburbs and streets; or they could research the history of the days of the week and the names of the months. Knowing the origins of these words can help students to understand and learn their spelling patterns.

Using Dictation

Dictation passages suitable for students who are using the word lists provided in the *Spelling Rules! Student Books Foundation, 1* and *2* are provided on **Reproducibles 2–7**. (The word lists themselves are also included in this book.) Advice on using these passages for assessment is included in the Assessing Spelling section on page 28.

Students might also be able to devise their own dictation passages using the list words and common high frequency words that they are reading. They can then dictate their sentences or passages to the class or to individual classmates.

The dictation passages on the reproducible pages can also be used by students in other ways. For example, students can give practice dictations to their peers; passages can be cut into individual word pieces and reassembled into sentences; and students can use them as models for their own writing. (It may be useful to enlarge the sheets to A3 for these activities.)

Students can also use the dictation passages as models to create their own books. For example, the dictation passage for *Student Book Foundation,* Unit 4 is 'Pat the cat'. Students could use this as a model and create a class book: 'Pat the crocodile/zebra/butterfly/alien/dinosaur/baby/kitten/zombie' and so on.

Dictation passages can also be used by students for handwriting practice. Neat and consistent letter shapes help in the development of visual knowledge of letter shapes and letter patterns in words. You can use the dictation passages to reinforce the conventions of writing in English – left-to-right direction of print, writing from the top of the page to the bottom, starting at the front of the book and using each page – and the concept that words are discrete units of meaning that require correctly formed letters.

You can also write dictation passages on the board, deliberately misspelling some of the words, and ask students to proofread them, either individually or as a whole-class oral exercise. Have students then write them correctly.

Using Cloze Passages

Cloze passages are a useful diagnostic tool for assessing spelling, as well as being useful in learning how to spell. In cloze activities, students use words within a context without needing to supply the context themselves. Cloze passages are an effective means of teaching phonics and spelling rules. Students can complete cloze exercises independently or working in groups.

When designing a cloze passage, make sure the first sentence is complete so that students can grasp the context. Alternatively, you can read the cloze to students, saying 'blank' where a word has been left out. This also helps students establish a context for the text.

Spelling Posters

Create word bank posters and charts based on theme or topic words for display and reference. Use these charts as a starting point to focus on a particular letter combination, for example *ough*. Write lists of words that contain the spelling pattern but are pronounced differently, for example *cough, through, dough*. Point out to students the different pronunciations.

Word Maps

Word maps enable students to explore particular aspects of words, liken the words to other words, focus on particular spelling features and so on. Word maps assist students in using analogy for spelling. Use theme or topic words as starting points for word maps. For example, if you are working on a unit on the ocean and a topic word is *fish*, a word map could look like this:

fisher

fishing **fish** fishes

fished

Or like this:

fish fish**ed** stepped / hopped / patted / jumped

Word Sorts

Use word cards that have been used for various purposes in the room. Have students work in groups to sort the words by a criterion of their choice (past tense, initial letter, final sound, verbs, number of syllables; any criterion is acceptable as long as students can show they have used it systematically in their sorting). Or choose a criterion for students to use.

Playing with Words

Enjoy word play with students. Use jokes, limericks, poems, riddles and so on, where the humour in words, sounds and other aspects of language can be appreciated by students.

Use transition activities where students need to suggest a rhyming word, or antonym or synonym, for example, to leave the classroom for lunch.

Games to Develop Spelling

Letter Cards

Reproducible 8 consists of a set of letter cards. These can be photocopied onto cardboard and covered with clear contact or laminated for long-term use. Students can use them for games such as the 'Letter by Letter' game or 'Mini Scrabble', listed below.

Flip Books

Write a focus letter combination for a word ending or beginning on a strip of cardboard, for example the word ending *un*. Staple on top of this more cardboard strips with beginning letters that work with the *un* ending. Students can flip through the book and make new words to write: *sun, run, bun, pun, fun, nun.* Or use the same procedure with a word beginning and a number of word endings: *unkind, unhappy, undress.*

Word Toss

Have students play in groups, using dice with letters stuck over the numbers. Tell them to take turns to roll the dice and make a word with the letters they have rolled. Students get one point for each letter used.

Snap

Create a deck of playing cards with words from student spelling lists written on the cards, one word to each card. Make sure that you have two or four cards for each word. Students can play this game in pairs, or in groups of three or four. Shuffle the deck and then deal each student an equal number of cards until all the cards have been dealt. Have students take turns placing a card face up on the table and spelling the word. When a pair is shown, the first player to spot the pair puts their hand on the pile while calling 'Snap!', then spells the word. The aim is to collect all the cards. When one player has the entire deck of cards, that player is the winner of the game.

Concentration (Memory)

Use 12–24 word cards made from cardboard, using words from student spelling lists, high frequency words or topic words. Shuffle the cards and place them face down, in rows, on a table. Have students play in groups of two, three or four. Each student turns over two cards, then reads and spells the words on the cards. If the cards are a pair, the student keeps them. If they are not a pair, the student turns them face down again and tries to remember where the words are. The next student takes a turn trying to find a pair.

The Letter by Letter Game

Playing the game 'Letter by Letter' reinforces how the spelling of a word is linked to how it is pronounced. Write a word on the board and ask students to change it, letter by letter, until it is a completely different word, for example *boy* → *toy* → *top* → *tap*. You could also use the alphabet tiles on **Reproducible 8**.

Bingo

Create bingo word cards using **Reproducible 9**. By laminating the cards and using wash-off marker pens or whiteboard markers, you can re-use the cards for each unit. Or you may choose to save the filled-out cards for revision and consolidation. Each card can include a letter or a list word on it, depending on the needs and developmental levels of the students. You can write the focus words or letters on the cards or students can choose and write their own words from the spelling list.

For a group of four to six students to play bingo, you'll need one card for each student. Each card should have a slightly different combination of letters or words to the others. Have one student call out the list words (or focus letters) one at a time. If students have that letter or word on their bingo card, they place a counter on it. When every letter or word on their card has been called, the student calls out 'Bingo!' and wins the game. For more capable students, use words that have very similar spelling so that students focus on the visual patterns in the words, for example *shoe, show, shone, shop, short, shore*.

An alternative is to ask students to copy six list words each from the week's list onto a bingo board. They must copy the spelling correctly, because if any words are wrong they will be disqualified from the game. Have another student call out and spell the list words in random order, until a player calls 'Bingo!'. A variation is to have that person then spell all their words correctly.

Alphabet Games

Students need to know their alphabet to find a word easily in a dictionary. Play alphabet games. Ask your students to arrange themselves in a line, alphabetically by first names, last names or middle names. Then ask them to arrange themselves alphabetically by the second letter in their first name, the second letter of their last name and so on.

Mini Scrabble

Photocopy and laminate two sets of the letters on **Reproducible 8**. Have students work in pairs or in groups of up to four. Each student is dealt six cards from the shuffled deck. Taking turns, students attempt to make a word with their cards. If they can make a word, they place it in front of them. Students get a point for each letter used, and replace their used letters with fresh cards off the deck.

A possible variation is to have students make their words connect to the words of other students, in the centre of the group. This is a little more difficult, but gives students access to an extra letter.

Students keep playing until all the cards are used, or until none of them can make any more words. They add their scores and subtract a point for each card they are left with.

Whispers

Play a game of 'Whispers' using tongue twisters. Divide the class into teams. Tell the leader of each team a tongue twister and ask them to whisper it to the next player in their team, who whispers it to the next player in line and so on. The last person in each team comes back to you and whispers the final result. Write what each team ends up with on the board and read them out to students.

Lists

Explore any opportunity to expand students' vocabularies and improve their phonological awareness. Play 'I'm Going Shopping'. Have students sit in a circle and take turns to name a shopping item using the last letter of the previous word, for example 'I'm going shopping and I'm going to buy bread–donuts–strawberries–sugar–rice . . .' Students need to remember all the previous shopping items in sequence. A variation is 'I went to the zoo and saw a lion–numbat–tiger . . .' (Note: do not use plurals or all animals will need to begin with s.)

I Spy

Play 'I Spy' using the first sound of the word, for example 'I spy with my little eye something beginning with *th*' (thumb). When learning final consonant sounds, say 'I spy with my little eye something that ends with . . .'

Flash Cards

Laminate blank A4 paper and cut each page into smaller cards. Use a whiteboard marker to write spelling words on the cards. Wipe off the words and re-use with each unit.

Students can use these cards in pairs or groups. Have one student say the word and the other student or students spell the words. This activity reinforces the learning of the words students are encountering in their spelling lists.

The flash cards can be used to play another form of spelling bingo. Deal out the cards to the class and then read out the spelling list, for example from the relevant student book. Tell students that when they hear the word for which they have the card, they should put it out in front of them. For this activity, a number of word cards will need to be made for each spelling word. A variation is to say 'Put out in front of you any words beginning with *s*' or 'that have the sound *t* at the end of the word' or 'that have the sound *o* in the first syllable'.

Rhyme Tag

Have students work in pairs. Ask them to take turns to say a rhyming word. The one who says the final word is the winner.

dog hog fog log flog cog slog frog jog bog

Word Webs

To reinforce the spelling of the words in the student books, play 'Word Webs'. Write a word on the board and ask a student to use a letter from the word to start or finish another. They could also use the letter as part of the middle of the new word. You should end up with a crossword-like structure on the blackboard. Students can then use the words to write their own sentences, or use a dictionary to find the meaning of words they don't know.

Puzzles

Puzzles such as anagrams (*time/item*), crossword puzzles, word worms, word squares and findawords are all good ways of supporting spelling. Have your students create word puzzles for the rest of the class to solve. Photocopy these and keep a supply to give to students as extension or supporting exercises, or to include as task cards in the spelling learning centre.

Word Square

blow in the wind

not hilly

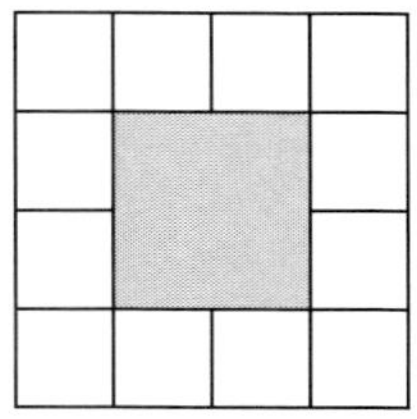

not work

he and she

Findaword

box, bat, open, nest, post, bend

b	o	x	o	s
b	p	o	s	t
e	e	e	p	f
n	n	e	s	t
d	b	a	t	o

For more able students, distribute the puzzle without listing the hidden words. Have students use different-coloured pencils to draw a line connecting the letters in the words they find. Ask them to write the words as a list below or beside the puzzle.

Word worms

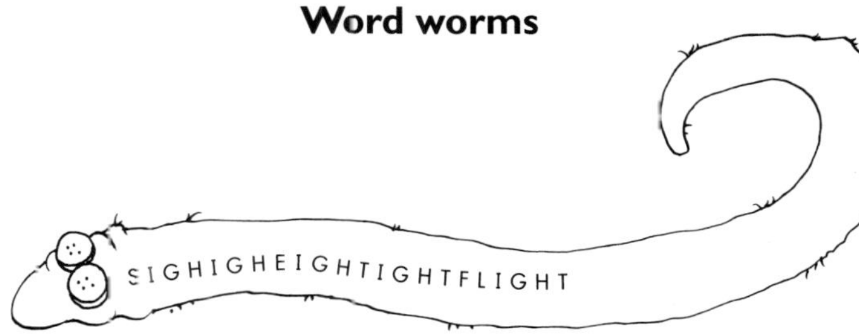

Students sort out the words in a string of letters. For more able students, the final letter or letters in one word should be the first letter or letters in the next word.

ASSESSING SPELLING

Why and How Do We Assess Spelling?

Spelling assessment needs to be conducted systematically and regularly. It can also take place spontaneously as opportunities arise during classroom literacy activities, including when you are modelling writing and in guided writing sessions.

The focus of assessment will be students' attitudes, skills and knowledge in spelling. You need to determine how students feel about themselves as spellers, whether they are confident to have a go at spelling, and what knowledge they are using when they attempt to spell (phonological, kinaesthetic, visual, etymological, morphemic or a combination of all). When looking at specific spelling errors, examining the type of error will determine the appropriate strategy to teach the student, or the knowledge base to extend or reinforce.

Accurate analysis of student progress in spelling facilitates planning for further spelling development in the teaching-learning cycle. Worthwhile assessment will be based on what has been taught and learnt, and should provide information about what needs to be taught next.

The Spelling Assessment Checklists (**Reproducibles 10–12**) are included to assist you in gathering assessment information systematically and recording this information for analysis and follow-up. The checklists cover the spelling skills, knowledge and attitudes dealt with in the *Spelling Rules! Student Books Foundation, 1* and *2.*

WRITING

Most spelling assessment opportunities will arise during the course of student writing. At these times, you can **observe** students' spelling, **interact** with them about their writing and spelling, and **collect work samples** for analysis.

Students' incorrect spelling *does* need to be corrected. Teachers sometimes worry that correcting spelling might undermine student confidence and have a negative impact on students' willingness to engage in writing and take risks with attempted spellings. It is important to keep student self-esteem in mind but it is also important to make sure that incorrect spelling does not become a habit. If students get used to writing and seeing a word spelt a certain way, that is the spelling that will stick, and it is not helpful to have incorrect spelling patterns enter the long-term memory.

SPELLING CONFERENCES

Spelling conferences enable you to discuss students' spelling with the students. Conferences can be conducted with individual students or with small groups of students who have the same spelling need at the time. You can share with students what you notice about the spelling and ask students what knowledge led them to make the spelling decisions.

For example, a student who wrote *elefnt* is using phonemic awareness and matching sounds to letters. During a spelling conference, you can point out that the /f/ sound can be made by the letter pattern *ph*. You can also give the student a mnemonic clue to assist with spelling memory by telling them to 'look for the tiny ant in eleph<u>ant</u>'. After a spelling conference like this, the student will probably remember the spelling of *elephant*. Record the outcomes of these spelling conferences in student folders, progress records or on student checklists.

Reproducible 13 provides a format for a general spelling conference.

WORK SAMPLES

Collect and date samples of students' work to analyse. Original drafts or photocopies can be collected in assessment folders. Writing samples can be compared from month to month to determine progress and development. The first work sample collected early in the school year provides a benchmark against which progress can be compared.

Dictation

Dictation passages are provided on **Reproducibles 2–7**. They will enable you to test the specific words being taught in the *Spelling Rules!* program. They provide the basis of a formal and systematic approach to assessment so you do not have to rely solely on incidental assessment situations. (See page 24 for more general ideas for using the dictations.)

A dictation passage can be used as an assessment of the week's work or as a diagnostic tool: use it as a pre-test to identify spelling problems prior to the commencement of the unit. Dictation passages can also be used to assess whether students are able to apply rules and conventions to unknown words and use analogy to work out spelling. The dictations can help you identify specific problems students may have in distinguishing sounds in words.

Follow a consistent procedure when dictating a passage. Read the whole dictation passage to the class, using appropriate intonation and expression. It is important that students understand the context, as the passage might contain words whose spelling will depend on the context (for example, homophones). Re-read the first sentence, breaking it into meaningful words, chunks or phrases as students write it down. Follow this procedure for each sentence, until you have finished the dictation. Finally, read the dictation again as a whole text and remind students to check their writing. It may be appropriate to give word meanings or encourage students to identify the parts of compound words, or prefixes and suffixes. Provide time for students to proofread their spelling and change anything that they need to.

After completing a dictation exercise, students should reflect on their own learning by making their own corrections. Older students can be asked to write their reflections on their spelling progress in their journals or learning logs. Student correction and reflection are integral parts of the learning process.

Dictagloss

While working on a particular topic or theme, you can read to students a text that includes the topic words that students are expected to learn, and ask them to write the **key words** as they listen. This is a similar exercise to note-taking. The object is not to write every word as it is dictated, but to listen for meaning and write the key words only. Read the text through twice and then allow time for students to reconstruct the whole text so that the meaning is clear and spelling is correct.

Cloze

Provide students with a text that has all the key words omitted but which can still be read and still makes sense. When constructing cloze passages, focus on particular kinds of words, for example topic words, high frequency words, verbs, nouns, pronouns, homophones, or combinations of any of these. Ask students to fill in the spaces in the cloze using correct spelling. A cloze passage provides a useful context for students' spelling and ensures that spelling is part of writing. It encourages students to bring all their spelling knowledge to the task and allows time for students to reflect on their spelling choices.

Peer Assessment

Students can proofread other students' writing. They can quiz each other's spelling and can also create written spelling quizzes, findawords, dictations and so on for classmates to use. Provide students with **Reproducible 22** to assist them with peer assessment.

Self-Assessment

Students can be encouraged to reflect on their own spelling, and can be involved in monitoring their own spelling progress. Reflection activities have been added to units in *Student Books 1–4*, to support self-assessment. **Reproducibles 13, 20 and 21** include spelling self-assessment formats for students to use when appropriate. Students can also record their thoughts and feelings about their spelling in their journals or learning logs.

Diagnosing Spelling Errors

English spelling is complex and many common words do not follow the rules and conventions taught. This can cause confusion for some students, as they may over generalise and have difficulty selecting the appropriate strategy for the target word.

When looking at students' work, it is important to acknowledge their efforts and recognise what they have achieved before focusing on particular errors. For example, if a student has written *cleen* for *clean*, recognise that he or she has selected an appropriate vowel digraph, as both ee and *ea* can make the long e sound. However, in this case the word is spelt like *mean* and not *seen*.

If the student is not attempting to spell some words, encourage them to 'have a go'. Positively support the student by pointing out what is right, and praise the student for what he or she can do. Review useful strategies and resources with the student, for example using a personal dictionary, picture dictionary, standard dictionary suitable for the student's age, topic word bank or list of frequently used words.

A written text may appear at first to have more words incorrect than correct. If this is the case, focus first on **the meaning of the text** and on **what has been achieved**, and then select a few words that you can work on together.

The following table gives examples of errors students often make in their writing, along with a brief analysis of the type of error and suggested teaching strategy.

Spelling error or concern	Analysis	Teaching strategy
mi for *my* *r* for *are* *lefunt* for *elephant* *hop* for *hope* *pn* for *pen*	Student is using the letter name instead of its sound.	• Reinforce the names and sounds of letters, e.g. the name of *n* is 'en', but in a word it makes the sound /n/. • Revise that some letters name themselves inside words.
elt for *elephant*	Student is spelling phonetically but is only able to hear initial and final sounds in the word. (Students are typically more able to hear the beginning sound of a word during early spelling development. They are usually next able to identify the final sound, and then sounds in the middle of a word.)	• Articulate all the sounds for the student so that he or she hears medial sounds. • Play games and transition activities where the student is asked to repeat medial sounds, e.g. short *o* sound in *shop*. • Teach that each syllable in a word needs a vowel or vowel digraph (including *y* when used as a vowel). Clap out syllables (e.g. three claps for *e-le-phant*) and make sure student can hear the separate syllables.
hot for *hat* *tap* for *tape*	Student is confusing pairs of words that differ only by one letter.	• Use minimal pairs to discriminate between sounds (e.g. *hat/hit, hat/hot, hat/hut, hit/hot, hit/hut, hot/hut*). • Use minimal pairs to explain how adding silent e changes the sound of a letter (e.g. *tap/tape, plan/plane*).
sum for *some* *eny* for *any*	Student is misspelling words that do not follow a regular spelling pattern.	• Explain that some common words do not follow the sound patterns they have learnt. • Suggest a mnemonic or ask the student to make up his or her own.

Spelling error or concern	Analysis	Teaching strategy
sed for *said* *dinu* for *dinner*	Student has not understood that sounds are not always represented by single letters.	• Teach non-CVC, high frequency words e.g. *said*. • Teach word families where the same digraph makes the same sound, e.g dinner, over, hammer, butter.
spagetty		• Explain that English has absorbed many foreign words and discuss the particular problem word and its origin. • Suggest a mnemonic or ask student to make up his or her own, e.g. *spag-hetti*.
mohter for *mother* *shcool* for *school*	Student has reversed the order of letters. Student is relying on (incorrect) visual memory rather than sound. Student is not sure of less common letter patterns (e.g. *sch*).	• Focus on developing accurate visualisation (see page 21 for ideas). • Check the student's phonemic awareness, review sound–letter representations and check student knows correct pronunciation of the word. • Ask the student to say the whole word aloud and then one sound at a time to reinforce sound–letter correspondence. • Teach/revise high frequency words.
the girl hirt hirself *school rools*	Student is over generalising by using the same letter pattern for all words with the same sound. Student is not aware of different ways of representing the same sound.	• Review different letter patterns that represent the same sound, e.g. *her, girl, turn*. • Group words that have the same letter/sound pattern, e.g. *her/term, girl/dirt/firm, hurt/fur/turn*. • Use mnemonics to help the student remember the different patterns.
leggs for *legs*	Student doubles letter unnecessarily in CVC word.	Remind the student that for words with a short vowel sound, the last letter is doubled when you add -*ed*, -*er*, -*ing* or -*y* but not when you add -*s* or -*es* to make a plural.
runing for *running* *funy* for *funny*	Student does not understand the rules and conventions of adding affixes to a base word.	• Teach/revise base words. • Review rules about adding affixes to base words.
mudy for *muddy* *shiney* for *shiny*	Student does not understand that when adding -*y*, the final consonant is doubled when the vowel sound is short, and the silent e is dropped when the vowel sound is long.	Review the rules for adding -*y* to a word ending in a consonant.
cald for *called*	Student is using a phonetic approach. Student is not yet able to analyse base word plus past tense morpheme.	Teach/revise common suffixes, especially different ways of pronouncing *ed* (/d/ as in *called*, /t/ as in *looked*, /əd/ as in *fitted*).
feeded	Student has regularised the irregular verb *fed*.	Teach that some words do not add -*ed* in the past tense e.g. *run/ran, write/wrote*.
happyly for *happily*	Student does not understand the rules for adding -*ly*.	Teach/revise that you change the *y* to *i* before you add -*ly*.

Spelling error or concern	Analysis	Teaching strategy
I wen to skool on mi yown.	Student is eliding final sounds in words so that they appear as initial sound in next word.	• Sound out words clearly for student. Make sure student is pronouncing all parts of the words. • Revise consonant blends such as *nt*. • Teach that the letter *y* can be a vowel as well as a consonant.
wonerful for *wonderful*	Student has written semi-phonetic version of word to match the poorly articulated version student hears.	Practise correct pronunciation of frequently mispronounced words, as whole words and as separate syllables.
their for *there* or *they're* *be* for *bee*	Student is confusing homophones.	• When correcting the incorrect use of a homophone, acknowledge that the word the student has written is correctly spelt but not correctly used. • Teach homophones and confusing words as contrasting pairs or groups. • Check that student understands the meaning and use of each word. • Explain the different word classes (e.g. *see* is what you do – verb; *sea* is where you swim – noun). • Suggest a mnemonic or have the student make up his or her own (e.g. *here* goes with *there* because you can see one inside the other).
of for *off* *were* for *where* *he's* for *his*	Student is confusing words with similar sounds and letters.	Practise auditory discrimination for pairs of similar-sounding words – see page 21 for ideas.
lisen or *lissen* for *listen*	Student has left out the silent letter.	Group words with the same silent letter together, e.g. *know/knew/knit/knot*.
icescream	Student has used sound instead of meaning to write a compound word.	• Teach/revise how compound words are formed. • Demonstrate how to break the compound word into parts as a guide to meaning.
cood for *could* *nite* for *night*	The student is misspelling more complex letter–sound representations.	• Teach rhyming word families, e.g. *would/could/should; night/fright/sight*. • Make up a mnemonic for common members of rhyming word families, e.g. *I would if I could but I'm not sure if I should!*
whent for *went*	Student is adding letters to words.	• Teach and emphasise proofreading strategies as the student may be writing too quickly to concentrate on all elements in a word. • Check whether the student is using analogy inappropriately, e.g. *whent* by analogy with *wh* question words.

Spelling error or concern	Analysis	Teaching strategy
teir or *ther* for *there*	Continued misspelling of high frequency words.	• Make a list of the high frequency words the student needs (personal dictionary). • Display high frequency words in classroom. • Use games. When reading a text, ask student to locate a specific high frequency word on the page within a set number of seconds or to count how many times a particular word occurs on a given page. • Look for words inside other words (e.g. *the, he, her* and *here* inside *there*). • Ensure that the student can say each word correctly to reinforce the sound–letter patterns. Break each word into its constituent phonemes (e.g. *th-ere, s-ee-n*) to reinforce phonemic awareness. • Ensure that each word is encountered at least 5–9 times to enable it to move from working memory to long-term memory.
skool, school, shool, scule	Student uses inconsistent spelling.	Model proofreading strategies.
downt for *don't*	Student is spelling contractions incorrectly.	Teach the full word or words from which the contraction is derived in order to identify the omitted letter or letters.
The book's are in the girls bag.	Student is misusing the apostrophe.	• Review -s as a plural suffix. • Explain that apostrophes are only used to indicate ownership and contractions.

Catering for the Struggling Speller

When spelling 'clicks' with students, they become increasingly better spellers very quickly and charge ahead of struggling peers at an exponential rate. The gap between their skills and those of the students who seem to make no progress – or very little – widens rapidly.

Struggling spellers need to experience success with spelling, so it is important to focus on what they can do in spelling and build on that. It is also important that their classmates recognise that all students learn at different rates and in different ways. Some students are better spellers than others, while some students are better at maths, others are better at athletics and so on. In a classroom environment, the ethos needs to be one of acceptance of differences, and no student should feel degraded or inferior. Students will model their attitudes on your attitudes, so it is important to model acceptance and to value the contributions all students make in the class.

Struggling spellers should only be required to learn a few words a day, focusing repeatedly on these words using the strategies provided below. With constant revision, these words can be retained in the long-term memory. It also helps if the words have similarities to each other, or to other words students have learnt, so that students can use analogy to assist their memory.

For some students, extrinsic motivation (stickers, stamps, praise) might be required, at least initially, until they start experiencing success. After this point, the success itself can become the intrinsic motivation necessary for the student to continue working at their spelling. Merit certificates are included on **Reproducibles 23–25**.

Never forget student interest as motivation. Take advantage of student motivation about certain topics to teach key points about spelling or to challenge students who need to be extended in spelling. For example, students will learn to read and sometimes spell dinosaur names because they're interested in triceratops and tyrannosaurus rex.

Where to Start

Begin with a thorough assessment of the student's current spelling ability. The spelling of students in the early phonetic or phonetic stages of spelling can be assessed using a test such as the one included on **Reproducible 14** and **Reproducible 15**.

Reproducible 14 shows all letters of the alphabet in random sequence. Ask the student to tell you the name of the letter and suggest a sound that the letter makes and a word that has that sound. Use the accompanying record page (**Reproducible 15**) to record student responses. For students in the early years of schooling in particular, this provides a good preliminary idea of what they know and what they don't.

Use **Reproducible 16** and **Reproducible 17** to assess the student's spelling of the digraphs and blends taught by the end of *Student Book 1*: initial *sh*, final *sh, ck, ll, st, sl, sm, th, ch, sk, sn, sp, cl, fl, pl, ss, nd, nt, ng, nk, ld, wh, oo, ou, ai, er, ow, ar, ay, oy, ir, or*.

Use **Reproducible 17** to record student responses. Show the student each word on **Reproducible 16**. Have the student read the word, then cover the word and ask them to spell the word. Record the student's attempts at reading and spelling, and your analysis of the student's mistakes. Try to determine which type or types of spelling knowledge the student is relying on. Use the 'Diagnosing Spelling Errors' chart on pages 30–33 to help determine where the student has gone wrong and to find useful strategies for assisting the student.

Use **Reproducible 18** and **Reproducible 19** to assess student knowledge of the letter patterns taught by the end of *Student Book 2*: *lk, kn, wr, mb, st, str, tch, sbr, scr, spl, thr, ew, oy, ay, ey, aw, oor, er, ir, or, ur, igh, ould, oa, ue, oi, ai, ie, ld*.

Use **Reproducible 19** to record student responses. Ask the student to read the words on **Reproducible 18**. Record whether they read the word correctly or what they said the word was. Next, ask the student to write the word and note if they remember the spelling. Try to determine which type or types of spelling knowledge the student is relying on. Use the 'Diagnosing Spelling Errors' chart on pages 30–33 to determine where the student has gone wrong and to find useful strategies for assisting the student.

You can also choose any of the word lists provided in this book or in the student books, and ask students to say the initial, final and medial sounds.

Useful Strategies for Struggling Spellers

All the classroom strategies previously mentioned are useful for struggling spellers.

If you have spellers who are struggling and you think that it might be helpful for them to build on their kinaesthetic perceptions, when students are using the 'look, say, cover, write, check' strategy, have them trace the letters with their finger as they say the word.

Experiment with grouping arrangements. Use volunteers, peer tutors, spelling groups and other arrangements to reinforce spelling. The partner or group games suggested in other sections of this book (see pages 25–27) are suitable for struggling spellers because they can be fun and take the emphasis off drill and exercise. Ensure that students can participate cooperatively in groups and are happy to work with other members of their groups.

Catering for the More Able Speller

Students who are more able spellers introduce a new set of issues to the classroom.

Common Questions about More Able Spellers

Should more able spellers be given word lists to learn, and if so which words?

Yes, they should, but at a more advanced level. Make sure you extend the more able speller rather than just giving them extra work at the same level.

Should they work from different student books to the rest of the class?

Yes, they should, if they have already achieved the skills and knowledge expected of the class text. Two or three students in a class working from a different student book can spend time together each day discussing spelling, and learning from each other.

Should they join a different group/class for spelling?

They can, if this is an option available in the school, and if the student, the student's family, the current teacher and the receiving teacher are all positive about the grouping arrangement. The school should expect the student to benefit from this arrangement beyond any benefits from remaining with the existing class group for the subject. Students can be allowed to join a different class for spelling if they have no spelling peers in their current class of age peers with whom they can be grouped for appropriate interactions regarding spelling. It is always useful for students to have opportunities to work with intellectual peers, no matter what the subject area. Socially and emotionally the student will need to be able to cope with the expectations of the different class. Alternatively, the student can be subject accelerated in his or her own classroom.

Do more able spellers still need to be taught spelling?

Yes, they do, beyond the level at which they have already demonstrated achievement. Students who are more able spellers can still make use of specific spelling instruction in areas where they have knowledge gaps, or to keep pace with their growing vocabularies. There are always spelling rules and exceptions that can challenge a speller. While more able spellers will still need to be taught about spelling, they will make analogies more quickly, form more connections and remember the words more readily than their age peers.

Can I have more able spellers help struggling spellers?

Yes, you can, providing that there is a benefit to both students, and that socially and emotionally both students are happy with the partnership. A struggling speller can sometimes make more sense of the way a more able speller communicates the spelling knowledge. Students who are more able can benefit from this arrangement both socially, in improved self-esteem and through working with peers, and scholastically; helping others can serve to reinforce and consolidate their own spelling understandings. However, do not rely on the more able speller to provide all of the support to the struggler.

Whether or not a more able speller will benefit from this form of interaction with struggling peers also depends on the personality of each student, and whether or not the more able speller regards it as a burden or a waste of their time, keeping them away from activities in which they would rather be involved. Use discretion and a consideration of all the factors when making any decisions regarding peer tutoring, and be willing to review any arrangements on a regular basis. At times, the struggling speller should be placed in the teacher role for spelling with younger or less able students, or in a different subject area.

Where to Start

A thorough assessment of what the student can actually spell and how the student manages the spelling task (what knowledge is already in place) is the place to begin with the more able speller, as it is with the struggling speller. In order to plan for any student, you first must find out what they already know.

Younger students can be given the same diagnostic tools as the struggling speller. A more able speller in the first year of schooling might know all common, regular letter–sound correspondences taught in *Student Book Foundation* but might not know some of the digraphs or blends taught in later units. You can assess students' knowledge of spelling patterns in blends and digraphs using **Reproducible 16** and **Reproducible 17**. These reproducibles assess the student's spelling of the digraphs taught by the end of *Student Book 1*: initial *sh*, final *sh, ck, ll, st, sl, sm, th, ch, sk, sr, sp, cl, fl, pl, ss, nd, nt, ng, nk, ld, wh, oo, ou, ai, er, ow, ar, ay, oy, ir, or*. Give the student **Reproducible 16**, which contains the words, and record student responses on **Reproducible 17**. For more detailed instructions on using these reproducibles, see pages 34–35.

Reproducible 18 and **Reproducible 19** can be used to assess student knowledge of letter patterns taught by the end of *Student Book 2*: *lk, kn, wr, mb, st, str, tch, spr, scr, spl, thr, ew, oy, ay, ey, ow, oor, er, ir, or, ur, igh, ould, oa, ue, oi, ai, ie, ld*. Give the student **Reproducible 18**, which contains the words, and use **Reproducible 19** to record student responses. For more detailed instructions on using these reproducibles, see page 35.

Using dictation passages, dictagloss activities and cloze passages as described on page 29 will also help you assess what a more able speller already knows.

Useful Strategies for More Able Spellers

Many of the strategies mentioned in 'The Spelling Classroom for Foundation to Year 2' (pages 20–27) are suitable for the more able speller, for example: spelling learning centres; computer programs and computer games; resources such as dictionaries; games and challenges; grouping with other more able spellers; and collecting riddles and jokes. More able spellers need spelling enrichment and extra challenge beyond age peers or class cohort so that they remain excited about spelling and don't get turned off by spelling that becomes drudgery. The following are useful enrichment activities.

Spelling Challenges

Have students compete with each other in a spelling challenge game. Call out words from revision lists or challenge lists. Have the student contestants write the word on the board or on paper for the rest of the class to see as soon as it is written. The first finished with a correctly spelt word earns one point. The first contestant to reach ten points is the winner. Students in the class could take turns to call out words. More able spellers could organise their own lists of challenge words, contributing 20 words each to the game.

Games

Students can create their own spelling games or use variations of spelling games such as the **bingo challenge**, a variation on bingo. Ask students to choose five spelling words from the word lists or class charts and to write these on paper. You can then call out clues such as *a word with four syllables, a compound word, a word with the long* e *vowel sound, a word that begins with* q, *a verb in the past tense*.

More able spellers might also be able to create the list of clues for you to use. These clues can also be used in timed challenges where students find as many words as they can to fit a particular clue in a certain amount of time, or more able spellers might be challenged to find three examples for each clue in the fastest time.

A Sequential Spelling Program

A sequential learning program is provided in the *Spelling Rules! Student Books Foundation, 1* and *2*. These student books contain weekly units of work for the first three years at school. It is suggested that *Student Book Foundation* is introduced in the second term of the first year at school, once other routines are settled.

The following notes include lists of skills to be taught in the first three years at school, scope and sequence charts, spelling word lists and useful strategies. Also included are week-by-week suggestions for classroom activities to enhance the learning of spelling.

The emphasis in the first few years at school is on developing students' interest in and understanding of print, letters, reading and writing, and developing positive attitudes about spelling and attempting to spell. Students need to have fun listening to the way words sound and having a go at spelling. They need opportunities to enjoy playing with language. Once students are writing texts of their own, they learn to value spelling as an asset to writing.

Activities to improve fine motor control and therefore handwriting are also useful in the first years at school: it is easier to develop visual knowledge in spelling when words are written consistently and neatly. One way to help students develop fine motor control is to provide pegs and have them peg their own art work out to dry, or use pegs for relay games (for example, each member of a team picks up a peg, runs a course and pegs the peg to a container at the end of the course to finish). Or provide coins for students to pick up and palm, picking up one coin at a time with forefinger and thumb, retaining them in their palm, and counting how many they can get inside their hand before they drop one.

Have students practise writing in their designated books or folders. Ensure that they use the correct pencil grip and know the movements and directions for forming each letter, and then, later, for joining letters. Students who need extra support can initially trace letter shapes, or you can provide them with dots to join to form the letter shape, or outlines of the letters to colour in.

Spend 10 to 15 minutes each day writing, revising and focusing on the list words so that students develop their ability to hear the sounds and see the letter patterns and begin to point out the sounds to you during conversations, stories and other activities, or notice the letter combinations in shared reading and in writing activities.

SPELLING RULES!

STUDENT BOOK FOUNDATION

Student Book Foundation

In the *Spelling Rules!* program, students will develop phonological skills by firstly learning letter names and sounds, and then learning common monosyllabic words. These words will have clear letter–sound representation, starting with consonant–vowel–consonant (CVC) words using short vowel sounds, and moving on to CCVC and CVCC words (like *ship* and *hill*), still using short vowel sounds.

The initial focus is on recognising individual letters and sounds. In general, three letters – two consonants and a vowel – are presented at a time in the program. The letters are grouped to ensure that the way they sound and look will not be confusing to students. Therefore, *b* and *d*, for example, are not presented together. For the vowels, the most easily identifiable sound is presented first and the sound that is most difficult to master is presented last. Finally, the letters are grouped so that whole words can be presented as soon as possible.

High frequency words that students need to use in their reading and writing but that do not have short vowel sounds (*be*) or that do not reflect a simple letter–sound relationship (*are, the*) are also included.

Skills Taught in Student Book Foundation

Phonemic awareness	Visual knowledge	Kinaesthetic knowledge	Letter–sound relationship	Proofreading
Recognising the different sounds of English Isolating sounds in words	Recognising letters from their shapes Recognising what a word looks like: the shape of the letters, combinations of tall, short or long letters	Recognising letters by tracing or writing their shapes Recognising what it feels like to write a letter or combinations of letters	Recognising the sound represented by a letter Being able to write a letter to represent a sound	Developing the skill of checking writing to ensure correct spelling is used

Scope and Sequence: Student Book Foundation

This scope and sequence chart is based on the requirements of the Australian Curriculum.

Unit	Page	Skill focus					
		Initial consonant	Initial vowel	Final consonant	Medial vowel	Consonant digraphs	High frequency/ sight words
1	4	s, t					
2	6	p	a				
3	8			p, s, t	short a		
4	10	c, g					
5	12	m	i				it, is, a
6	14			g, m	short i		am, at
7	16	d, l			short a, i		do, did
8	18	n	o, a	plural suffix s			no, as, on
9	20			d, l, n	short o		not, got, so
10	22	REVISION and high frequency/sight word: I					
11	24	b, r					
12	26	h	e				an, he, she, me
13	28			b	short e		him, my, by
14	30	REVISION and high frequency/sight words: his, her, new					
15	32	f	u				us, or, one
16	34	j, k					be, we, the, to, go, are
17	36			f	short u		of, if, put
18	38	REVISION and high frequency/sight words: and, said, you					
19	40	**CVC words; minimal pairs; high frequency/sight words: for, our, out**					
20	42	q, v, w, y, z					was, will
21	44			x			went, very, school
22	46	**Upper- and lower-case letters**					
23	48			long y as vowel sound			why, this, that, boy
24	50			plural suffix s			any, many, two, how
25	52	REVISION					
26	54					initial sh	shoe, now
27	56					final sh	want, have, your
28	58					ck	were, does, what
29	60			double l			
30	62	REVISION OF UNITS 1–29					
31	64					initial th	them, they, four, here, when
32	66					final th	good, some, where

Word Lists: Student Book Foundation

Unit	List Words	Extension Words
3	pat, sat, tap	tramp, sand, stand
4	cat, cap, gap	camp, cramp, gasp
5	mat, map, it, is, sip, pit, in, a	mist, must, happy
6	sit, pig, tip, tag, am, at	big, stop, stag
7	dig, lip, lap, dip, do, did	lips, lamp, maps
8	no, nap, nip, as, on, pal, cats, dogs	snap, snip, man
9	tin, not, got, pot, log, nod, dot, pod, so	spot, mum, ball
10	pin, lid, dad, can, man, sad, tan, pop, I	slid, love, spin
11	bat, big, bin, rag, rip, rod, rat, bag, bit	brat, brother, sister
12	has, had, an, hat, hot, egg, he, she, me	ham, leg, beg
13	rib, red, bed, ten, get, pet, him, my, by	rob, blob, slob
14	bad, net, top, his, hid, hit, her, men, new	glad, stop, today
15	fat, fan, fin, fit, up, us, or, one, fog	until, under, over
16	jam, jog, job, be, we, the, to, go, are	kiss, kick, kit
17	of, if, mum, sun, run, bus, fun, hug, put	sift, soft, swift
18	jug, fed, mad, but, hug, leg, and, said, you	fist, first, mug
19	pan, jet, hip, cot, bug, for, our, out	pot, pet, cost
20	van, wet, web, yes, zip, zoo, yet, was, will	queen, who, wall
21	six, fix, mix, box, fox, wax, went, very, school	sock, rock, shock
23	fry, fly, why, try, cry, sky, this, that, boy	sly, sty, dry
24	lots, any, many, see, two, how	more, less, show, number
26	shy, ship, shop, shut, shed, shoe, now, sell, shoes	hush, crush, lush
27	wish, wash, push, fish, cash, rush, want, have, your	crash, dish, splash
28	back, duck, neck, sick, sock, shock, were, does, what	tick, tock, clock
29	hill, shall, doll, bell, fell, yell, all, call, well	pillow, yellow, follow
31	then, them, they, thin, thick, three, four, here, when	chin, stick, trick
32	with, bath, both, moth, path, tooth, good, some, where	mouth, teeth, there

Useful Strategies

Introduce letters and letter combinations by their most common sounds. Students will eventually need to learn all the sounds made by all the letters, but it is useful to begin with short vowels and readily distinguishable consonants such as *s*, *t* and *m*. When each new letter or group of letters is introduced, say the sounds of the letters out loud for students. Have students repeat the sounds.

Start each lesson in *Student Book Foundation* with a discussion of the banner and the letters hidden inside. Ensure you point out to students the focus of each activity as it is introduced, for example initial, final or medial sounds, rhyme, colour-coding, drawing lines from letters to pictures and so on.

Ensure that students can write all the letters that you have been focusing on in class and can instantly say their sounds.

Have students:

- look at the shapes of letters or words as you write them
- make the letter shapes with their fingers, with play dough, and with seeds and other collage materials
- write the letters in the air, in sand, on paper or the board
- cut the letters out of magazines to make a collage
- work with a partner using their bodies to make the letter shape
- sort magnetic focus letters from the rest of the alphabet by sight or by feel (in a 'feely' bag)
- play a mix-and-match game with upper-case and lower-case letter cards, or use these cards for snap games
- play hopscotch with letters – as students hop through the grid they have to say the names of the letters, the sounds the letters make or a word that starts with each letter
- unscramble letters to make words
- look at each other's mouths and lips as they say letter sounds such as the *p* sound to ensure that the sounds are made correctly
- learn and sing the alphabet song
- play sound bingo. Students use bingo cards with pictures on them, placing a marker on all the pictures that start with the sound you say
- listen to the placement of the sound in the word. Ask students whether the sound is at the beginning of the word, at the end or in the middle
- do picture and letter matching activities. Draw or collect pictures and on separate pieces of paper write the letters that make the first sounds of those words. Mix them up and ask students to match them. Be careful about judging a student wrong with their letter choice until you have asked them what the picture is
- help you create shared class stories that make use of focus words or spelling patterns. Publish the stories as class books and allow students to take the books home to 'read' to their families.

Assessment

At this stage, students should be showing an interest in sounding out words and writing letters. They should be able to write or copy their names. They might be able to write and recognise most letters of the alphabet. Assess each student individually to determine their ability to identify sounds in words.

Revision opportunities occur at Units 10, 14, 18, 25 and 30 in *Student Book Foundation*. Identify students who will benefit from revision as well as those who do not require revision but who would benefit from extension activities.

Some students might need extra practice in making and writing the letters, to reinforce their shapes and sounds. Other students might be able to copy words from the word lists and make their own books. It is always important to respond to students' individual needs.

Spelling Focus: Initial consonants **s, t**

Student Book Foundation **Unit 1**

Ask students to describe what they see in the unit banner. Write their suggestions on the board or chart paper, for example *snail, shell, leaf, grass, eyes, eye stalks, smile.* Have students use coloured pencil to trace over the s and *t* shapes on the pages of the student book and identify the s at the end of the snail's trail. You might also like to point out the rhyme in 'snail's trail' to help focus student attention on the sounds in words.

Write the letters *t* and s for the students to see. Say the sounds of the letters to students. Have them repeat the sounds. Ensure that you do not voice the sound of either letter. These letter sounds are made by escaping air – they do not use the voice.

Ask students to suggest words they know that have s and *t* sounds in them.

Create a word list that uses the letter s, for example *sausages, snakes, sneeze, snot.* Cook a sausage sizzle, buy jelly snakes as a treat, paint pictures of sneezes and display them in the classroom under a sign that says s *is for sneeze.*

Create a word list that use the letter *t,* for example *teddy, tea, toast.* Have a teddy bear's picnic and serve toast and pretend tea. Take photos and create a class book. Vote on whether or not teddies would like tomatoes, tacos or television. Write a class book of instructions about teddies cleaning their teeth.

Have students practise writing the letters.

Spelling Focus: Initial vowel **a**; initial consonant **p**

Student Book Foundation **Unit 2**

Tell students to used coloured pencil to trace around the **a** and **p** shapes in the illustrations in question 1.

Have students who are able label the illustrations in the unit: *astronaut, pear, pencil, arrow, anchor, prince, ant, pumpkin, plate, axe.* Say the words slowly with students. Stretch the words out to emphasise the *a* and *p* sounds. Some students might comment on the *a* sound inside *plate* but you really want to focus student attention on the short *a* sound at the beginning of the words at this stage.

Say the sounds of the letters *p* and *a* to students. Have them repeat the sounds. Ensure that you do not voice the sound of the letter *p*. This letter sound is made by escaping air – like a puff – without using the voice. Ask students if they know the names of the letters, but focus on the sounds at this stage. Point out that the letters *a* and *p* face in opposite directions.

Some students might know that *a* is used on its own to make a word and that when it is a whole word on its own it is pronounced differently, making the indeterminate 'schwa' sound as, for example, in the phrase 'a pig'.

Have students practise writing the letters *a* and *p*.

Help students create alliterative sentences using the vocabulary in the unit. For example, *Andy Ant is an astronaut; Polly Pig ate a pumpkin off a plate.*

Select students to illustrate the sentences. Alternatively, you could ask peer tutors from upper grades or parent helpers to assist.

Write the sentences on cardboard and cut out each word. Have students reassemble the sentences.

Spelling Focus: Final consonants **p**, **s**, **t**; medial vowel short **a**

Student Book Foundation **Unit 3**

Have students practise writing the words in the boxes.

Ensure that students know how to listen for and write the last sound in the words.

Make a chart in the room for colour words and write each word in its appropriate colour (for example, red should be written in red), so that students can refer to the chart when asked to colour letters in their student book.

Some students will be able to learn to spell each of these words. Focus their attention on the spelling of *the* as a high frequency word.

Tell students that they will need to say and listen to words to hear the sounds at the end of the words. Say these words to students, first at normal speed and then slowly, and ask them to repeat the final sound of each one as they hear it: *goat, flop, cap, hiss, step, map, cat, sat, sip*.

Ask students to suggest words that end in the sound of the letter *s*, then *t* and then *p*.

Write *rat* on the board. Ask for a student volunteer to change one of the letters in the word to make a new word, for example *pat*. Continue until students have run out of suggestions.

Say the following words to students one at a time and ask students to stand if they hear the *a* sound in the middle of each one: *pig, cup, cap, tap, rat, sun*. Ask students to suggest words of their own that have the *a* sound in the middle.

For writing practice, ask students who are capable to copy this sentence: *The red rat ran in the sun and got hot.*

Spelling Focus: Initial consonants **c**, **g**

Student Book Foundation **Unit 4**

Point out the word *a* in the sentence *I see a cat in a cap*. Point out how it makes a different sound from the *a* inside *cat* and *cap*. Tell students that it is a whole word on its own.

Ask students to brainstorm words that start with the same *c* sound as cat. Write the words on chart paper. Choose some and create a crazy cat story. Begin the story *Once there was a crazy cat called Connie*. Exaggerate the hard *c* sound. Ask students to take turns to add the next sentence to the story. Tell them to put as many hard *c* words as possible in the story. If students say words that start with *k*, use the words, but as you write you can point out which words start with *c* and which ones start with *k*.

Brainstorm words that begin with a hard *g* sound.

Create alliterative chants for hard *c* or *g* and clap the rhythms in syllables. For example,
Crazy Connie met a cranky crocodile.
Giggly Gus has gone to get a goat.

Show students how to write *c* and *g*. Have them practise writing these letters and CVC words using the letters they have covered so far: *c, g, s, t, p, a*.

Eat grapes for morning tea. Paint a large bunch of grapes and have each child copy a *g* word onto an individual grape. If they are not able to copy, give them a dot pattern to trace.

Spelling Focus: Initial consonant **m**; initial vowel **i**; high frequency/sight words: **it, is, a**

Student Book Foundation **Unit 5**

Point out the monster at the top of the page and the letter *m* on its back. Paint pictures of monsters and write *m* to display with the pictures.

Make a map to the monster's hideaway.

Look at the letter frames for the tall, long and short letters (page 13). Make sure students understand the differences. Do some with the whole class on the board first.

Write *map* and *mat* on the board. Ask students, 'What's the difference?'

Make the letter *m* in the air with students.

Read pirate stories. Practise talking in pirate voices. Make treasure maps for pirates. List all the things that could be in the treasure chest.

Show students how to draw a treasure map, then let them create their own maps and pictures of treasure. Have them copy the word *map* onto their paper.

Students capable of doing so should be encouraged to copy the word *treasure* and to sound out the word and look at the spelling pattern. They can also have a go at the word *pirate*.

Discuss the initial *i* in the words *it* and *is*. Point out that in the word *is* the *s* makes the *z* sound. Brainstorm a list of words that start with *i*.

Revisit all word charts and lists around the room. Ask students if they remember how to spell any of the words written on the lists.

Place plastic letter shapes *c, g, s, t, p, i, a* inside a bag such as a pillowcase. Have students take turns to place their hand inside the bag and choose a letter, name it and bring it out of the bag to see if they are right.

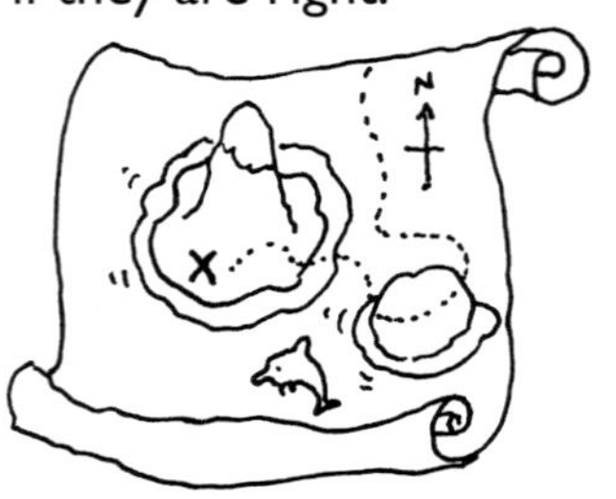

Spelling Focus: Final consonants **g, m**; medial vowel short **i;** high frequency/sight words: **am, at**

Student Book Foundation **Unit 6**

Ensure that students understand that they need to write the *final* sound for each picture: *drum, ham, dog, bag, arm, jug, pig, leg, jam*.

Explain how to colour the circles and squares for whether the sound is at the beginning or end of the word. Practise on the board so that students get the idea.

Make *m* and *g* sounds with students. Point out the way the lips create the *m*. Point out the way the hard *g* sound (as in *leg*) is made in the throat.

Write the list words *sit, pig, tip, tag, am* and *at* on the board. Ask students to spell the words, name the letters and point out any features of the words that they can think of. For example, students might suggest that *sit, pig* and *tip* have *i* in the middle; they might use analogy to say that *sit* looks like *sat* except for the *i*; they might say that *pig* ends like *dog* and so on.

Ask students if they can hear *g* at the beginning of the word or the end of the word in these words: *log, goat, pig, dog, got, green, jug, grab, great, dig*.

Ask students if they can hear *m* at the beginning of the word or the end of the word in these words: *pram, monkey, money, make, Tom, meat, team*.

Write CVC words on the board and ask students to fill in the blanks, for example *p_g, d_g, m_t, m_p, s_t, s_p, s_m, t_m, l_g*. Ask students to think of some for themselves. A challenge for capable students could be to make a list of all the three-letter words they can write.

Spelling Focus: Initial consonants **d**, **l**; medial vowel short **a**, **i**; high frequency/sight words: **do, did**

Student Book Foundation **Unit 7**

Discuss rhyme with students. Write the following two columns of words and show students how they rhyme, and how to join them with lines when they do rhyme.

pig	sip
tip	dig
big	lip
hip	rig

Make the *l* sound with students, focusing on where in the mouth and throat the sound is made. Brainstorm all the words students can think of that contain the *l* sound, for example *like, love, look, lemon, little, Lily, Lucy*.

If a student in the class has a name beginning with *l*, make up a tongue twister. Ensure that it is positive and will benefit the child's self-esteem, and ensure that you do not stereotype by gender. For example, *Lovely Lucy likes little lizards. Lovely Lenny likes to laugh.*

Rehearse the tongue twisters as action rhymes. Exaggerate the *l* sounds. Make an action for each syllable in the tongue twisters. For example, *Love-ly* (with two claps) *Lu-cy* (two finger clicks) *likes lit-tle* (slap knees with hands three times) *li-zards* (two head nods, one to each side).

Make up an action rhyme tongue twister for each student in the class. Divide the class into small groups and have each group learn the action rhymes of its members. Perform for another class.

Write *dig* on the board and ask students to change one letter at a time to make new words, for example *dig, dog, dot, pot, pat, sat, sit* etc.

Spelling Focus: initial consonant **n**, initial vowels **o**, **a**; medial vowel **i**; plural suffix **s**; high frequency/sight words: **no, as, on**

Student Book Foundation **Unit 8**

Make sure students understand that the shapes of the boxes on page 19 show the shapes of the letters that go inside. Practise some on the board for the following words: *nip, nap, am, a, pat, sat, dog, log*.

Students should now recognise the letters *s, t, a, c, g, m, i, l, d*. For revision, say with students the letter names and the sounds they have learnt for the letters so far.

Write *nip* and *nap* on the board. Ask students what the difference is. Rub out the middle vowels and show students that the words look the same. Ask students what the words mean. Have students make the *n* sound and notice the vibration in their mouths and inside their heads.

Have students write *n* in the air and on paper and then practise writing the other letters they have learnt.

Brainstorm *n* words, for example *nest, net, neck, necklace, nasty, nice, nana*.

Use vegetable dye to dye dried pasta tubes red, blue, green or other colours of your choice. This will need to be done the day before you want to use it. (Don't leave the pasta too long in the dye or it will get soggy.) Make small coloured cardboard shapes such as squares, circles, diamonds. Write letters on the shapes for the names of students in the class. Students can thread coloured pasta and their name letters to make hanging decorations or jewellery. Some students might wish to make something for a member of their family.

Point out that s can be added to naming words to mean more than one. For example, *1 dog, 2 dogs*.

Spelling Focus: Final consonants **d, l, n**; medial vowel short **o**; high frequency/sight words: **not, got, so**

Student Book Foundation **Unit 9**

The owl at the beginning of the unit has a letter *o* for its body but the *o* in *owl* is actually used with the *w* to say *ow*. You can write *owl* for students to show them when *o* does not say its usual sound. Tell them people say 'ow' when they get hurt. Suggest they draw a picture of someone getting hurt and write 'ow' in a speech bubble.

Make a list of rhyming words for 'ow': *cow, now, how, bow, wow*. Have student role-play situations where someone gets hurt and says 'ow'. Have students role-play situations where someone says 'wow'.

Write some *Do not* . . . signs for the classroom using the symbol on page 21 – the circle with the cross through it. For example, you could have *Do not feed the fish. Do not run inside. Do not make a mess. Do not shout.* Have students copy the *Do not* . . . words and finish the sentence for themselves.

Write the following on the board and read with students: *on, og, od, ot, op, om, ol, on*, focusing student attention on the *o* sound. Ask students to suggest a letter that could go at the front of each one. List these underneath each other.

Point out that when words sound the same at the end, it's called *rhyme*. Say *dog, log, fog, hog, mog, tog, zog, pog, nog*. Use nonsense words and focus on the rhyming patterns in the words. After playing with rhyme, ask students to suggest which ones aren't actually words that mean something, and wipe those off the board.

Write these words on the board: *in, pin, lid, can, man, sad, can, tap, sit, sat, pan, dot, mop*. Draw word frames on the board and ask students to write letters in the right box shapes to make words from the list. Read the words with students. Sound them out.

Ask students to copy the following sentence onto paper and fill in the missing letters. Tell them to read the sentence to themselves and then draw the picture: *A s_d d_g s_t on a l_g*.

Spelling Focus: Revision and high frequency/sight word: **I**

Student Book Foundation **Unit 10**

Write *pin, lid, can, man, sad* on the board. Ask students to say the words, then spell the words. Ask them to suggest rhyming words for any words on this list. Play any of the spelling games suggested on pages 25–27 of this book.

Spelling Focus: Initial consonants **b**, **r**

Student Book Foundation
Unit 11

Check that students understand how to complete question 6, the rhyme activity.

Say the words *bat, big, bin* to students. Ask them what sound they hear at the beginning of the words. Have students repeat the words after you. Try saying *ba, be, bi, bo, bu* because *b* on its own is difficult to make a sound for. It's made with the lips and escaping air, but without using the voice.

Make butterfly prints by placing blobs of different colours of paint in the middle of a sheet of art paper and then folding the paper in half, squishing out the paint and then opening the paper out to dry. Use a thick black felt-tip pen to draw the outline of the butterfly wings and a body. Glue on coloured pipe cleaners for antennae. Display with a sign that says *beautiful butterflies*.

Focus students' attention on how the *r* sound is made by curling the tongue back and having the sides of the tongue pressed against the teeth. Ask students to suggest words that start with the *r* sound: *robot, rabbit, red, rich*.

Have students work in pairs or groups of three to construct robots using boxes and any craft or construction equipment available. Ask them to bring recycled materials from home (but not toilet paper rolls, for hygienic reasons). Allow them to work on their robots during the week. Tell them to give their robots names starting with *r*. They could introduce their robots to an assembly and walk on and off like robots themselves.

Spelling Focus: Initial consonant **h**; initial vowel **e**; high frequency/sight words: **an, he, she, me**

Student Book Foundation
Unit 12

Explain to students that in question 1 they need to say the words out loud and listen to hear whether e or *h* is the first sound of the word.

Explain the spelling rule that says that *an* is used in front of words starting with the letters *a, e, i, o* or *u*, and *a* is used before all other letters.

For example:

an apple, an egg, an igloo, an orange, an umbrella

a dog, a cat

An exception is *a unicorn*, because *unicorn* starts with a consonant sound.

Point out that *a* makes a grunt sound (the indeterminate vowel sound, as in the phrase 'a pig') not the *a* sound in *cat* when it is used as a small word, on its own.

Focus words this week include *has, had, an, hat, hot, egg, he, she, me*. Point out the visual and phonological features of the words. For example, *egg* has a double g; the s in *has* says z as in *zoo* (like in *is* and *his*).

Point out that by changing one letter in *hat* it becomes *hot*.

Write *The h_n h_s _n _gg*. Ask students to fill in the missing letters. Point out the full stop at the end. Point out the upper-case *t* that starts the sentence. Ask students for suggestions for words that rhyme with *hen* – for example, *hen, pen, den, men, ten, when, then* – and write them underneath *hen* in a column. Circle *en* and make sure students can recognise the rhyme.

Create a visual display: brainstorm words that have the short e sound, write them on eggs and sit them in a nest with a hen on top.

Show students the spelling of *he, she* and *me* and point out that they rhyme with *tree* and *we*. Point out also that *she* has a *he* hiding in it.

Spelling Focus: Final consonant **b**; medial vowel short **e;** high frequency/sight words: **him, my, by**

Student Book Foundation **Unit 13**

Check that students can sound out and read the words at question 5. Write the words on cards and ask students to place them into rhyming pairs. Ask them to think of words to rhyme with any that don't have a pair, and to write these on cards for themselves.

The list words for the unit are *rib, red, bed, ten, get, pet, him, my, by.* Write the words on the board. Read them with students. Ask students to tell you which words rhyme (*red/bed, get/pet*). Add more rhyming words to the list.

Use as a model for students' own writing the sentence *Dan has a dog for a pet.* Ask them to write the sentence onto a sheet of A3 or A4 art paper but substituting the word *dog* with a different animal of their choice, and then draw a picture. Compile their pages into a class book. Choose a student to create a cover for the book and write the title. The authors can write their own names on the cover page.

Encourage students to be as crazy as they like with their choice of pets and point out the spelling features of the pets they choose. Remind them to use upper-case letters for names and the beginning of sentences, and full stops at the end of sentences. Some students might be interested in writing more than one sentence. These students can write more detailed stories about pets.

Write words for the numbers 1–10. Display the words with their numbers and with the correct number of dots or items. Make a class number book. Choose items for each number and collect pictures from magazines or draw the items.

Spelling Focus: Revision and high frequency/sight words: **his, her, new**

Student Book Foundation **Unit 14**

Question 1 includes an illustration of a spinning top. Make sure students know what a spinning top is. You could bring pictures or a real top to the classroom.

Question 6 asks for opposites. Work with students to explain opposites – *good/bad, hot/cold, sweet/sour, empty/full, tall/short, top/bottom.* Use the words in sentences so that students understand the vocabulary used.

Spelling Focus: Initial consonant **f**; initial vowel **u**;
high frequency/sight words: **us, or, one**

Student Book Foundation
Unit 15

Show students how to find little words inside bigger words, for example *at* in *fat*, *in* in *fin*.

Introduce the letter *f* and the sound it makes at the beginning of words: *fat, fan, fin, fun*. Focus student attention on the position of the top teeth on the bottom lip when making the *f* sound. Make sure they do not voice the sound – the *f* sound is just a soft, escaping air noise.

Ask students to suggest other words that start with the *f* sound, for example *finger, fish, flip, flop, family, funny*. Practise saying this tongue twister: *Five funny fish flopped on their fins*. Make sure students exaggerate the sound of the *f*s. Some students might like to create their own *f* tongue twisters.

Introduce the letter *u* and the common short sound it makes in words. Draw a picture of some undies on the board. Point out that the word *undies* starts with *u*. Give students a photocopied outline of a pair of undies and ask them to design their own colours and patterns inside.

They can use fluoro, polka dots, stripes, pictures of pigs, whatever they like. You might like to allow them to use paint or crayon resist. They can write the word *undies* on their art work for display.

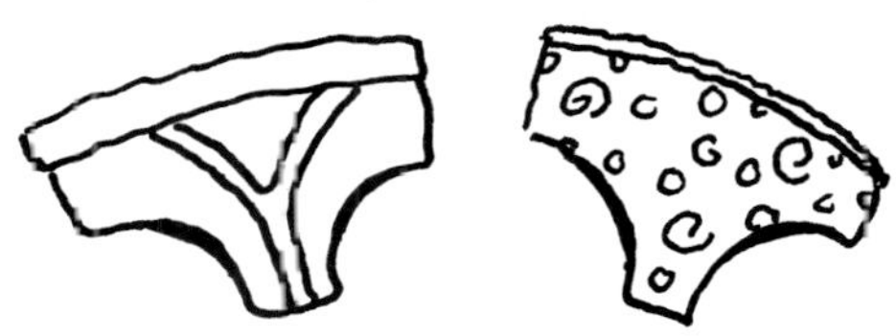

Spelling Focus: Initial consonants **j**, **k**;
high frequency/sight words: **be, we, the, to, go, are**

Student Book Foundation
Unit 16

Say the words *jam, jog* and *job* for students. Write them on the board. Point out that the words start with the letter *j*. Have students say the words. Ask them to suggest other words that start with *j*. Make jelly in class or bring jelly from home for students to eat.

Make up a chant about jelly or jellyfish. Ask students to help you. Practise the chant with actions, for example:

Jiggly, jolly jellyfish

Sitting on a rock,

Jiggled, joggled, juggled,

Plopped, plopped, plopped!

Students need to learn the word *the* and how it is often pronounced with a grunt. The grunt, called the 'schwa' or indeterminate vowel, can be heard in words such as pat<u>ie</u>nt, creat<u>u</u>re, li<u>o</u>n, doct<u>o</u>r – it is the vowel sound of most unstressed syllables of English.

The vowel sound in *the* makes this grunt when the word that follows *the* begins with a consonant: *the pig, the dog, the cat*. *The* rhymes with *me* or *we* when it comes before a vowel: *the apple, the egg, the umbrella*. When reading story books and big books, point out *the* when you read it so that students recognise how frequently it is used.

Rewrite some of the classroom labels to include *the*, for example *the art cupboard, the teacher's desk*.

Write the following sentences on the board and ask students to write in the missing list words.

Kick ________ ball.
I can get a ________.
I can eat ________.
We like to ________.

Play bingo with the list words.

Spelling Focus: Final consonant **f**; medial vowel short **u**; high frequency/sight words: **of, if, put**

Student Book Foundation
Unit 17

For question 6, it is important that students understand the connection between the beginning and the ending of each sentence. Write sentence beginnings and sentence endings and ask students to read them, use logic and connect them appropriately. For example: *I will pat the dog/if it is friendly. I will eat dinner/if I am hungry. I will swim/if it is hot.*

The list includes two words that use final consonant *f* (*of, if*) but the final *f* does not make the same sound in both words. Say the words *of* and *if* for students. Ask them what sounds they hear the *f* make. The *f* in *of* actually sounds like a *v*. Use *of* in a sentence for students, for example *I drank a cup of milk*. Write the sentence.

Write *off* for students and point out that the double *f* says the same *f* sound as in *if*. Write a sentence for students to demonstrate *off*. For example: *Hop off the bus. Mum got off the bus.* Point out the upper-case letters and full stops when you write sentences.

Paint a big mural of a bus and have each student write a sentence about themselves and draw a self-portrait: *Jett got off the bus. Vishaak got off the bus. Miyu got off the bus.* Have them cut out their self-portraits and glue them to the mural.

Read the other list words to students: *mum, sun, run, fun, hug, put*. Ask students to say which words rhyme, then ask them for further rhyming words.

Another sentence to write for students is *I give my mum a hug*. Ask students to copy the sentence onto paper and replace *mum* with some other word, or replace *hug* with another word that still makes sense: *I give my dog a hug. I give my mum a bug*. Display and discuss their sentences.

Spelling Focus: **Revision** and high frequency/sight words: **and, said, you**

Student Book Foundation
Unit 18

Play bingo with these words for revision: *bag, beg, big, bug, bat, bet, bit, but, jog, jug, fit, fat, lips, sun, leg, sad, cot, dad, men, and, if, of, off, the, said, you.* Write the words on the board. Distribute copies of the bingo word card on **Reproducible 9**, and tell students to select six words each and copy them correctly onto the card. Choose a student to stand at the board and call out the words in random order and spell them.

As the words are called, students who have them written on their card tick them off. The first student with six words ticked calls out 'Bingo!'. That student has the next turn at standing at the board and calling out and spelling the words. Alternatively, make pairs of cards with the revision words written on them and have students play snap.

Spelling Focus: CVC words; minimal pairs; high frequency/sight words: **for, our, out**

Student Book Foundation
Unit 19

The format of question 5 is new for students, so ensure that they understand that they need to choose the word that will make sense in the sentence.

Further examples:

The cat lost his/him ball.	*My mum is hat/hot.*
Mum lost she/her cup.	*My dad sat/cat on the mat.*
My pet is a rat/hat.	*The rat lost him/his cap.*

Write the following words on the board: *pan, jet, hip, cot, bug, beg*. Read them with students. Ask students to change a letter in each word to make a different word, for example *pen, jot, hit, cat, bag, big*. They can do this in pairs at their desks.

Have students work in pairs to choose a letter from each group of letters on the right and make as many CVC words as they can.

n f b d l g r p s t m c j	e u o a i	d t p n m s k b g

Spelling Focus: Initial consonants **q,v,w,y,z**; high frequency/sight words: **was, will**

Student Book Foundation
Unit 20

Use the sentences in question 6 as models and have students write their own sentences: *Liam's cat has a fluffy tail.* Make a class book. Point out the use of upper-case letters for sentence beginnings and full stops for sentence endings.

List words for this unit are *van, wet, web, yes, zip, zoo, yet, was, will.* Read the words to students and focus their attention on the sounds for the letters *v, w, y* and the shape of the mouth when you make these sounds.

Write *q* words on the board, for example *quack, quiet, quarrel, quit, quill, quaint*. Ask students if they notice something about the *q* words. (They all have *u* after the *q*.)

Also write z on the board or chart paper and make a list of z words, for example *zoo, zebra, zinc, zany, zigzag*. Say the z sound with students. Point out that you use your voice to make the z sound. Ask them to notice the vibrations in the mouth as they say *zzzzzzzzz*. Brainstorm words that end in zz – *buzz, fuzz, fizz*, etc.

Write this sentence and say it with students: *The zippy zebra zigged and zagged.*

Make *yes/no* reversible signs using ice-block sticks and small paper plates. Write *yes* on one side of the sign and *no* on the other. When students all have a sign, ask them questions that require yes or no answers, for example *Is 'cat' spelt c-a-t?*

Discuss words that rhyme with the list words. List them according to spelling patterns. For example, – *who, moo, boo, grew, flew, blew, zoo, too, sue, to, shoe*. Use each of the words in a sentence for students so that they can hear all the words while they look at all the letter patterns.

Spelling Focus: Final consonant **x**; high frequency/sight words: **went, very, school**

Student Book Foundation **Unit 21**

Cover a box in coloured wrapping paper and then make a chain of *x* words to hang from it in the room.

The list words for the unit are *six, fix, mix, box, fox, wax, went, very, school.*

Point out the *ks* sound at the end of the words ending in *x*. (The word *socks* has the same *ks* ending, but it is spelt differently. The *ks* sound at the end of *socks* is due to the *s* that is used because the word is plural.)

With students, make lists of words that are spelt with an *x*, for example *Max, tax, hex, saxophone, fax, next, text.* Say all the words slowly with students so that they hear the *ks* sound in the words.

Have students play word toss. You'll need five dice. Write letters of the alphabet on small stickers and attach these to cover the numbers on the dice. Have students play in groups of three or four. Ask them to take turns to roll all the dice and make a word with the letters rolled. They get one point for each letter used.

Spelling Focus: **Upper- and lower-case letters**

Student Book Foundation **Unit 22**

Have students copy and finish the sentence *My name is* ________________.

Make cards for upper- and lower-case letters and ask students to work in pairs to match the letters.

Play a memory game with the alphabet cards where students need to find the upper- and lower-case pairs.

Discuss with students when to use upper-case letters: for proper names (proper nouns) like people's names or the names of pets and the names of cities, towns or countries, and for the start of sentences.

Spelling Focus: Final consonant long **y** as vowel sound; high frequency/sight words: **why, this, that, boy**

Student Book Foundation **Unit 23**

Teach students the question mark symbol. Point out that it is used for writing questions. Give students some sample statements and questions and ask them to tell you whether or not each one is a question.

It is hot.

Is it hot?

Is that my hat?

Why have you got my hat?

Ask students to make up their own questions and statements.

The list words are *fry, fly, why, try, cry, sky, this, that, boy.* In addition to learning the sound of *y* as a vowel at the end of these words, students will also be learning *sk, st, tr* and *wh*. Ask students for other words that rhyme with the rhyming list words, for example *dry, pie, die, my*.

Make a class book: *We cry* . . . or *I cry* . . .

Have students write sentences to explain when they cry. *We cry when we fall over. We cry in a sad TV show. We cry when we are sorry.* Have students illustrate their sentences, then collate them as a class book. You could also use the sentences for role-play.

Play the 'Letter by Letter' game. Write a word on the board and ask students to change it, letter by letter, until it is a completely different word. For example, *box* → *fox* → *fix* → *fit* → *sit*.

Ask students to make word worms for their friends to solve. Have them write strings of letters with words hidden inside, for example *youknowyessftwettvanmto*. Their friends need to find the words.

Spelling Focus: Plural suffix **s**; high frequency/sight words: **any, many, two, how**

Student Book Foundation **Unit 24**

Count items in the classroom or around the school and compile a chart of statistics. For example:

There are 10 classrooms in the school.

There are 270 children in the school.

There are many trees in the school.

A list word for the unit is *many. Many* deals with numbers of things. Write synonyms for many (*some, heaps, stacks, lots, masses*) and antonyms (*few, hardly any, none*).

Focus students' attention on the spelling of *many.* Point out the word *any* inside *many* and that the *a* makes the short e sound. Ask students to suggest sentences that use the list words or other words that indicate amounts.

Remind students that by adding s to a word, one item becomes more than one. Show students written examples, such as *1 cat, 2 cats, 3 cats, 4 cats* and so on.

Compare this with *There are many cats.*

Ask students when we would use the word *many* instead of an exact number.

Review the words for numbers. Write and read the numbers from one to ten. Play matching games with the number cards made earlier at Unit 13.

Have students make name posters for their own names. Write each child's name, making each letter shape a large outline that students can fill in. Tell students they can decorate their names with any colours or types of collage or art material they choose. Display their art in the classroom. Examine some of the spelling patterns in the names. Discuss the origins of the names, for example *Alejandro* (Spanish), *Vishaak* (Indian), *Akari* (Japanese). Display the names on a world map or in groups according to country of origin.

Spelling Focus: Revision

Student Book Foundation **Unit 25**

Play spelling noughts and crosses. Players must spell a revision word suggested by an opponent in order to be allowed to place a nought or a cross on the grid.

Spelling Focus: Consonant digraph initial **sh**; high frequency/sight words: **shoe, now**

Student Book Foundation **Unit 26**

Make sure students recognise the pair of shoes revealed when they colour question 2.

Remind students of how to find small words inside big words, for example *she* inside *shed*.

Play a memory game. Write the nine list words (*shy, ship, shop, shut, shed, shoe, now, sell, shoes*) on cards. Place the cards face up on a table or on the floor in the centre of the group. Have students look at the words and say the words. Cover the words and take one word away. Uncover the words and ask students to name and spell the missing word.

You'll need A4 size letters for this game. (Large foam rubber alphabet tiles are commercially available for classroom activities, or you can make your own tiles and either laminate them or cover them with clear contact.) Place letters on the floor in random order. Have students play in teams. All the students in each team have to cross to the other side of the river using the letters as stepping stones. They must make words as they jump or leap from letter to letter. The first team to reach the other side is the winner. You could also play this game as a relay.

Write a long list of letters (word worm) on the board and embed list words in it, for example *nshedhshoppshoeishylpship*. Ask students to volunteer to come to the board and underline the list words. Have students create a spelling challenge of their own using words of their choice for classmates to solve.

Spelling Focus: Consonant digraph final **sh**;
high frequency/sight words: **want, have, your**

Student Book Foundation **Unit 27**

The *sh* letters in this week's list words can be used to indicate 'Be quiet'. Write *sh* on five pieces of cardboard. Ask students to work in five groups to make up short dramatisations that freeze when they get to the point of holding up the *sh* sign. To get them started, ask students to think of situations when they have been asked to 'Sh!' or be quiet – near a sleeping baby, in class, when other people are watching TV and so on. Have students make up plays in their groups and freeze when they get to the *sh*, holding up the *sh* sign.

Read the list words (*wish, wash, push, fish, cash, rush, want, have, your*) to students. Ask students to read the list words and tell you what they notice about any of the words. They might suggest the sounds they make, the letters they are made of, that some include *sh* and so on.

Read the word *wash* to students. Tell them that the *a* makes an *o* sound in this word and the best way to remember how to spell it is to pronounce it to rhyme with *mash*.

A memory trigger could be saying 'I mash my clothes as I wash them.'

Another tricky word in this week's list is *push*, where *u* says *oo* as in *look*. Ask students to think of ways to remember how to spell *push*. Perhaps they can chant 'I push the pram through the mush' and pronounce *push* to rhyme with *mush*. Using memory triggers like these is a useful way to help students learn tricky spellings.

Spelling Focus: Consonant digraph **ck**;
high frequency/sight words: **were, does, what**

Student Book Foundation **Unit 28**

Have students look at the drawing of the shocked person on page 58. Ask students what aspects of his face make him look shocked. Discuss facial expressions in real life, in cartoons and in picture book illustrations. Ask students to find picture examples of facial expressions to show others in the class. Discuss how we can 'read' the meaning of facial expressions.

Read the list words to students: *back, duck, neck, sick, sock, shock, were, does, what*. Point out that the two letters *c* and *k* make one sound together. Ask students to suggest rhyming words for each of the list words.

Discuss the meaning of the word *shock*. Discuss the sorts of things that would give someone a shock. Would the same things shock a friend as a mum, a dad, the teacher, the principal? Write a class book. Have each student contribute one page. They can choose who their page is about and what sort of shock the person should get. Have students fill in the missing words to complete their sentences.

____________ *got a shock when*____________.

Students who need an extra challenge could write more than one sentence and elaborate on their story.

Read the book to the class. Allow students to borrow the book to share with their families. Students might like to work in groups to dramatise some of their suggestions.

Play a game based on unscrambling the letters in words. Students can work in teams of three or four. Each team is given the same set of scrambled word cards. The first team to unscramble all their words and write the words correctly wins. Students could make up their own sets of scrambled words to use in the game, but you need to check that the words include all the letters they need.

Spelling Focus: Double consonant ll

Student Book Foundation **Unit 29**

Make use of nursery rhymes such as *Ding, dong, dell, Pussy's in the well* to have fun with language and reinforce aspects of rhyme for students.

Read the list words with students (*hill, shall, doll, bell, fell, yell, all, call, well*) and point out the sounds of the double *l* and the words that rhyme.

Play letter toss. Draw a grid on chart paper for the floor, like the example below. Write letter combinations that students have learnt inside each square on the grid. Students take turns to toss a coin onto the grid and then must spell a word that contains the letter pattern. They score a point for their turn if correct.

sh	m	l	o	n
h	ck	g	i	d
b	qu	y	e	f
j	x	q	a	r
k	p	c	u	st

Spelling Focus: Revision

Student Book Foundation **Unit 30**

Have students make up tongue twisters about themselves. Use parent helpers or volunteers to help students publish their sentences using correct spelling.

Choose one student's name and have students compete to make as many words as they can using the letters in that name.

Read the following sentences to the class and then ask students to proofread them:

tom hass siks ducs

it iz hoot inn ther son

jen haz u pett ratt

Students could write the correctly spelt versions in their books. Note whether students remember to use upper-case for names and the beginning of sentences. Also note whether they remember the full stop at the end of a sentence. The correct versions are:

Tom has six ducks.

It is hot in the sun.

Jen has a pet rat.

Have students play word sort: students are given cards containing a number of their revision words. They then have to sort the words by letter patterns or sounds. They can be asked to determine their own criteria, for example words with double *l*, words with *sh*, words with *ck*.

Spelling Focus: Initial consonant digraph **th**; high frequency/sight words: **them, they**

Student Book Foundation
Unit 31

Read the list words *then, them, they* and then read *thin, thick, three*. Discuss the different sounds made by *th* in the two sets of words. Point out to students that the two letters *th* work together to make one sound in each of the words. Have students practise saying the words and tell them to notice how their mouths feel when making the different sounds.

Read *four, here* and *when* with students. Make sure students realise that four is a number word. Write the sentence *I had an apple for lunch.* on the board. Point out the spelling of *for* and the way it is used in the sentence. Ask students to suggest other sentences that use *for*.

Write the question words *who, what, where, when* and *why* on the board. Tell students that questions often begin with these words. Ask students to make up questions beginning with any of the *wh* words. For example: *When will we go home? Where do you live? Who do you live with?*

Write the questions on the board and point out the question marks. Make sure students understand that questions ask for answers. Have students state answers for the questions.

Point out that *thick* and *thin* have opposite meanings. Brainstorm and list other words with opposite meanings. Create an illustrated class book of opposites.

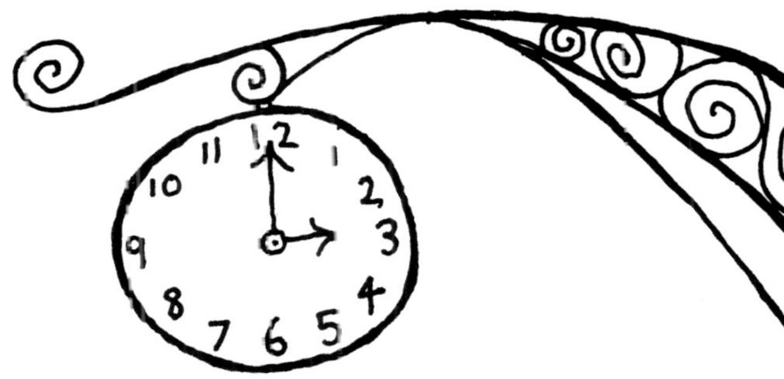

Spelling Focus: Final consonant digraph **th**; high frequency/sight words: **good, some, where**

Student Book Foundation
Unit 32

Read the words with students. Ask students what they notice about the spellings of the words. They should notice that the *th* in *with, bath* and *both* is the same as *thin, thick* and *three* in the previous unit.

They might point out the *oo* in tooth. Ask students to think of words that have this same sound. Write them for students to see. For example, *shoe, glue* and *chew*. You could also point out that *oo* makes different sounds in *look, cook, hook, book* and *booth, roof, spoon*.

Students should also notice that *where* is a question word. Point out that *here* is in *where*. Use this as a mnemonic to help students remember how to spell *where*. Discuss how the beginning sound of *where* is made with two letters: *wh*. Have students brainstorm words that begin with this sound, or revise words they have previously learnt that begin with the *w* sound.

Write the words in two columns: those that begin with *w* and those that begin with *wh* (*wish, will, win, wash, wet, was, web, we, wax, were, went* and *why, white, who, what, why*).

Use the *wh* question words to explore a narrative that you have read to the class. Ask *who* the story is about. List the characters. Ask *where* and *when* the story is set. Ask *what* went wrong for the characters and *why*. (This is the complication.) Ask *what* events took place and *what* happened in the end. (This is the resolution.)

Show students how to use the question words when planning their own story writing. Jointly construct a class story.

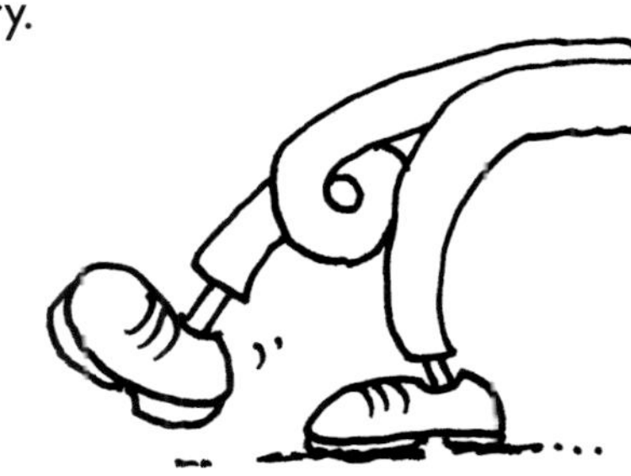

SPELLING RULES!

STUDENT BOOK 1

Student Book 1

In Year 1, the emphasis is on further developing students' interest in and understanding of print, letters, reading and writing. Continue to emphasise correct pronunciation and recognition of the sounds in words, and the relationship between the sounds and the written letters that represent those sounds.

Student Book 1 supports the development of positive attitudes about spelling and attempting to spell. Spelling should be fun and students should find it an exciting yet achievable challenge to listen to the way words sound and have a go at spelling.

The student book provides students with opportunities to expand the core vocabulary of sight words that they are likely to need when reading or creating their own written texts. Words that students may need or that they find interesting in their own reading and writing can be recorded in the spaces in the student book or in students' personal spelling books or personal dictionaries.

In *Student Book 1*, students are introduced to simple spelling rules and conventions. They are taught to apply their knowledge of rules and conventions to enable them to spell words that are similar to the targeted words, thus using the skill of analogy. Students are also encouraged to focus on the visual appearance of a word to aid in spelling memory.

Revision opportunities occur at Units 6, 12, 18, 24, 30 and 35.

Skills Taught in Student Book 1

Phonemic awareness **Letter–sound correspondence**	**Visual knowledge**	**Kinaesthetic knowledge**	**Morphemic knowledge and** **Etymological knowledge**
Developing further knowledge of sound–letter representations, spelling patterns and the pronunciation of sounds Developing an understanding of syllabification as a strategy for assisting spelling Developing an understanding of rhyme	Extending vocabulary of high frequency sight words, including subject-specific words Using personal or published dictionaries Recognising words by the way they look Using analogy	Recognising what it feels like to write letters and combinations of letters in words Recognising what it feels like to pronounce letter sounds and combinations of letter sounds	Developing an understanding of word families Using base words with suffixes such as *-ing* Learning simple irregular plurals such as *fish* and *children* Building compound words Using analogy Developing an understanding of homophones

Scope and Sequence: Student Book 1

This scope and sequence chart is based on the requirements of the Australian Curriculum.

		Skill focus				
Unit	Page	Vowels	Consonants	Letter patterns	Homophones/Confusing words	Topic words
1	6	short sounds	digraphs			
2	8	ee, short oo				
3	10		ll			
4	12		st			
5	14		sl, sm			
6	16	REVISION				
7	18			er		family words
8	20		short y as vowel sound	double letters		
9	22	a-e, e-e				
10	24	i-e, o-e, u-e				
11	26		ch		irregular plurals	
12	28	REVISION				
13	30		sk, sn, sp			
14	32		cl, fl, pl			
15	34	long oo				
16	36		s, ss			
17	38		nd			
18	40	REVISION				
19	42		nt		of/off	
20	44	ou				
21	46		br, cr, dr, gr, pr, tr			
22	48			ow		
23	50		ng			
24	52	REVISION				
25	54		nk			
26	56	ea			be/bee, sea/see, bean/been, meat/meet	
27	58			ar		
28	60			ay, oy	to/two, by/buy	
29	62			ir, or		
30	64	REVISION				
31	66				one/won, to/two/too, four/for, eight/ate	numbers 1–10
32	68		ld, silent t			
33	70	ai			stare/stair, sail/sale	
34	72		wh			
35	74	REVISION OF UNITS 1–34				

Word Lists: Student Book 1

Unit	Simpler Words	List Words	Extension Words
1	dip, sip, pop	hip, hop, ship, shop, dish, fill, shell, pack, wish, luck	quack, sack, quick
2	beg, fit, hop	see, bee, feet, sheep, queen, look, book, foot, good, wool	wood, would, should
3	pill, bill, ill	all, ball, tall, wall, fall, bull, full, pull, walk, talk	chalk, stalk, shall
4	top, pen	stop, step, stick, rest, best, fast, list, lost, must, last	past, pest, post
5	sip, lid, sell	slip, slop, slap, slug, slid, sleep, slim, asleep, small, smell	stall, steep, slime
7	mum, dad, me	his, her, mother, father, brother, sister, taller, smaller, baby, family	grandmother, grandfather, uncle
8	belly, dotty	jelly, silly, happy, funny, sunny, puppy, sleepy, wobbly, body, very	foggy, pretty, furry
9	a, at	ate, cake, bake, take, late, gate, date, game, name, here	tame, blame, flame
10	hid, rid, slid	like, hide, smile, fine, toe, nose, hole, hope, stone, rude	glide, tune, whole
11	hop, hat, chip	chin, chop, chat, chips, child, children, chase, rich, much, such	lunch, bunch, sheep
13	snip, pin, nip	spin, spine, snap, snake, snack, skip, skin, skate, wasp, desk	sport, spade, sneeze
14	log, late, cub	fly, flat, flag, clap, club, clock, plate, plan, plant, place	float, plane, clown
15	moo, boo, too	zoo, pool, room, moon, boot, roof, tooth, food, spoon, school	fool, choose, teeth
16	must, rest, rust	pass, mess, kiss, moss, fuss, class, grass, dress, plus, minus	cross, plus, loops
17	land, band, man	end, send, hand, sand, kind, wind, pond, stand, grandmother, grandfather	wand, grand, spend
19	pen, pant	ant, want, went, sent, spent, tent, bent, hunt, aunt, uncle	off, of, blunt
20	out	our, loud, cloud, house, mouse, shout, mouth, found, round, about	mountain, fountain, ground

Unit	Simpler Words	List Words	Extension Words
21	trim, brim, drag	tree, crab, frog, from, pram, drive, grape, green, broom, friend	fiend, truck, train
22	yell, how, sow	owl, mow, cow, how, slow, show, grow, down, brown, yellow	growl, prowl, bellow
23	ring, sing, ping	hang, bang, king, bring, thing, song, long, hung, sting, swing	singing, swinging, beginning
25	No simpler words	ink, pink, wink, sink, think, drink, bank, thank, drank, skunk	slink, stink, drinking
26	No simpler words	eat, ear, sea, meat, bean, leaf, near, each, beach, clean	teach, meet, been
27	far	arm, car, park, dark, star, start, hard, barn, smart, farmer	war, wart, harm
28	by, day	say, play, stay, tray, today, away, boy, enjoy, toy, buy	yesterday, holiday, enjoying
29	No simpler words	bird, girl, stir, dirt, shirt, fork, torn, short, sport, more	thorn, third, ladybird
31	No simpler words	one, two, three, four, five, six, seven, eight, nine, ten	won, too, o'clock
32	No simpler words	old, cold, gold, told, sold, hold, held, bald, build, world	listen, often, should
33	No simpler words	air, hair, chair, tail, sail, snail, train, wait, stair, said	stare, snare, fingernail
34	whip	who, why, when, where, what, which, wheel, whale, white, wheat	whether, weather, whisper

Useful Strategies

In Year 1, students can be presented with longer lists of words to explore. Encourage students to use the words in their own writing so that spelling becomes embedded in the context of writing. Be cautious about turning students off spelling with exercises where, for example, students are always obliged to write list words in sentences. Tedious exercises such as these can discourage students from enjoying the challenges and excitement of spelling.

In Year 1 students will develop more sophisticated strategies to assist spelling memory so that they do not need to rely so heavily on phonological awareness. These strategies include:

- focusing on visual differences in words
- focusing on meaning to determine spelling, especially with homophones
- using analogy, especially rhyme and alliteration
- using mnemonics
- consistently using 'look, say, cover, write, check'
- learning how to proofread
- publishing written work
- using personal word books consistently.

Using *Student Book 1*

Each unit has a word list. There is space provided for students to practise writing each word, as well as a *My own words* box for students to write other words they are reading or learning that they find interesting and useful.

It is important that all students are encouraged to attempt spelling independently and that they feel a sense of accomplishment for giving it a try. Praise students when they attempt to spell words independently, even if these words are not spelt correctly. Point out to students the parts of a word they got right and the strategies they used successfully, and congratulate them for this. Use the Merit Certificates on **Reproducibles 23–25** as extrinsic praise for students' efforts in spelling.

Encourage proofreading as a good habit. When students have completed an activity, encourage them to check their work and to make changes where necessary.

When helping students to edit their work, look first at the whole text and the meaning the student is trying to communicate. Then look with the student at the mechanics of the text – the grammar and spelling.

Each unit in *Student Book 1* begins with a reminder for students to SLLURP. SLLURP is an acronym that summarises the strategies that will help spelling move from working memory to long-term memory. SLLURP also relates to the icons that go with each activity. SLLURP helps to remind students to do the following: **S**ay the word carefully and slowly to yourself, **L**isten to how each part of the word sounds in sequence, **L**ook at the patterns of letters in the word and the shape of the word, **U**nderstand the relevant rules, word meanings and word origins, **R**emember similar words you can already spell and relate this knowledge to the new word, and **P**ractise writing the word until it is firmly fixed in long-term memory.

Assessment

Assess students' understanding of the knowledge presented in *Student Book Foundation* using **Reproducible 14** and **Reproducible 15**. Some students may be beyond this level already. Use **Reproducible 16** and **Reproducible 17** to assess students' knowledge of blends and digraphs.

Revision opportunities in *Student Book 1* occur at Units 6, 12, 18, 25, 30 and 35. Identify students who will benefit from revision as well as those who do not require revision but who would benefit from extension activities.

Spelling Focus: Short vowel sounds; consonant digraphs

Student Book 1
Unit 1

Point out to students the heading **S**ay **L**isten **L**ook **U**nderstand **R**emember **P**ractise **(SLLURP)** above their list words. Explain to them what the reminder means.

Question 7 requires students to write about their favourite toyshop. Brainstorm the vocabulary students might require before they start writing. Make a chart of words they might need. Use pictures from toy catalogues and have students make a wish list ready for birthdays. Make a class book with months of the year, and for each month include students whose birthdays fall in that month, plus their wish list of birthday presents.

Write the list words on the board or a chart. Read the list words with students. The words revise spelling patterns covered in *Student Book Foundation*: short vowels *a, e, i, o* and *u* and digraphs *sh* and *ck*. Ask students to suggest other words with these spelling patterns, or words that rhyme.

Spelling Focus: Vowel digraphs **ee**, short **oo**

Student Book 1
Unit 2

Learn to recite *Little Bo Peep* as a whole class rap or chant.

Little Bo Peep

Lost her sheep

Where can she look?

. . . and so on. Say the words with students. Point out the ee and the *oo* sounds.

Play a game of word scrabble on the board. Write a list word and ask students to take turns to write other list words that connect. Students could also be asked to write words that rhyme with any of the list words. For example,

```
s h e e p
        e
        e
        p
```

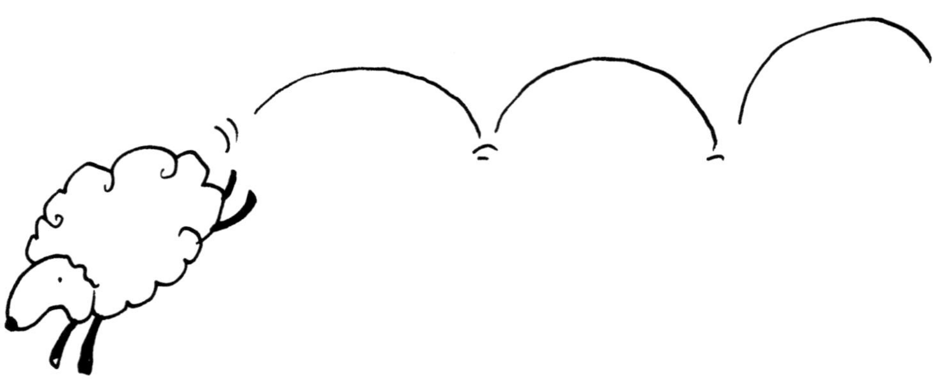

Spelling Focus: Double consonant **ll**

Student Book 1
Unit 3

Explain to students how to make the word walls in question 3. Challenge students to create their own word walls and ask peers to solve them.

Say the words to students. Write *all* on the board and then say rhyming words: *ball, tall, wall, fall, small*. Make sure that students can all hear the individual sounds in the words. Point out the way the *a* sounds inside of the words. Ask students to count the sounds and count the letters and compare. For example, *wall* has three sounds and four letters.

Write *bull, full* and *pull* on the board. Say them to students and point out the sound the *u* makes in the words. Ask students to think of other words that have this sound inside them, for example *push, look, good*.

Teach students how to recite the rhyme *Humpty Dumpty* as a rap or chant. Older students from a senior class could be recruited to help. Create a class poster with the words and illustrations for the rhyme.

Point to the words as students rap. Students could add some percussion to their rap. You can extend the rap by giving Humpty Dumpty some lines:

Yo, what's wrong with you all? I had a fall.
Fell off that wall. Did not bounce like a ball!
Went splat like an egg and broke off my leg.
Crying shame, and now I'm lame!

Students can all practise saying Humpty's lines, with rapper attitude, and then perform for another class.

Spelling Focus: Consonant blend **st**

Student Book 1
Unit 4

Question 2 answers *star, nest* and *stool* are not list words. Some students could be challenged to learn the spelling of these words for extension.

Read the list out with students, then sound the words out. Say *last* and *fast* with an American accent (that is, with a short *a* sound) and tell students saying the words with an accent will help them remember the spelling. Write *nasty, mast, past, grass* and look at the spelling with students. These can also be pronounced with a short *a* sound as a memory aid.

Write rhyming words for the other list words: *rest/best/pest/test/nest; stop/plop/flop; list/mist/fist; must/dust/rust/gust*.

Write the following rhyme on chart paper for students to learn. Point out the many rhyming words and the spelling patterns that students have already learnt.

Ms Polly had a dolly who was sick, sick, sick.
She called for the doctor to come quick, quick, quick!
The doctor came with a bag and a hat
and she knocked on the door with a rat-a-tat-tat.
She looked at the dolly and she shook her head.
She said, Ms Polly put her straight to bed!
She wrote on a paper for a pill, pill, pill.
I'll be back in the morning, yes, I will, will, will.

Teach the rhyme to students, then practise saying it slowly, quickly, with sad voices, with happy sing-song voices, with pirate accents, and any other ways that students suggest. Perform for another class. You could also change the main characters: *Mr Jolly had a polly* . . .

Spelling Focus: Consonant blends **sl, sm**

Student Book 1
Unit 5

Students are asked to differentiate between *sm* words and *sl* words. Ensure that students are pronouncing these sounds clearly. Focus on the way the mouth makes the sounds, and practise the sounds in any other words students can think of that have *sm* and *sl*.

Discuss the illustrations at question 7. Ask students what they can see and what they might write. Remind students that sentences start with capital letters and end with full stops.

Write *slip, slop, slap* on the board. Wipe out the medial vowel in each word so that students can see that the other letters remain the same. Pronounce each word clearly with students so that they hear the sound of each letter as you point to it on the board.

Write some of the list words with scrambled letters and ask students to unscramble them.

Slip, slop, slap can be used to remind students to be safe in the sun.

Ask students what they notice about the words. Another word to add to the sun-safe message is *wrap* – meaning to wrap round some sunglasses to protect the eyes from the sun's harmful rays. Have students make sun safety posters including the words *slip, slop, slap* and *wrap*. Have them role-play being lifesavers at the beach or local pool, reminding people to take care of their skin.

Point out the ee in the words *sleep* and *asleep*. These words rhyme with *sheep* and *peep* explored in a previous unit.

The spelling of *small* also has a letter pattern that students have used before – *small* rhymes with *all, tall, ball, wall, fall*, which were covered in Unit 3.

Spelling Focus: Revision

Student Book 1
Unit 6

Write colour words in correctly coloured paint or felt-tip pen: *red, blue, pink, green, purple, yellow*. Display them in the classroom so that students can refer to them for question 1. *Slip* is the word that is not coloured.

Teach students about compound words before they attempt question 3.

Have students draw and label their own pictures like the one in question 4, using words they have learnt in previous units.

Spelling Focus: Digraph **er**; topic words: family

Student Book 1 **Unit 7**

Ensure that students understand the family relationships in the illustrations on page 18. Discuss the illustrations with the class.

Seven of the list words contain *-er: her, mother, father, brother, sister, taller, smaller*. Write the words on the board and read them to students. Ask students to comment on other spelling features of the words. Look for smaller words in the words, for example *her* in *mother* and *brother*; *tall* in *taller*; *moth* in *mother*; *fat* and *her* in *father*; *small, mall* and *all* in *smaller*.

Show students how to write *mummy, daddy, granny, grandpa, aunt, uncle* and other words for their family members. Write *family* and *baby* for students to read. Point out that both words end in the short *y* sound.

Have students create *My Family* posters. They can draw a family portrait, add photos of family members and write the names of their family members and their titles; for example, *Sho's Family: Mummy, big sister Arisa, little brother Riku, me*. They could also use photos of family pets or holidays and any other information that they would like to share with the class. Students could seek help from home to write out information about themselves and attach it to their posters, for example cultural background of family, languages spoken at home, favourite food, favourite game to play, things I'm scared of, things that make me happy.

Have students clap out the syllables in all the list words and in other words on display in the classroom. Ensure that they recognise that syllables match the beats in a word. Some students might understand that syllables need to contain a vowel sound and usually start with a consonant.

Spelling Focus: Short **y** as final vowel sound; double letters

Student Book 1 **Unit 8**

Read the list words with students. Discuss the short *y* sound made by *y* at the end of each word. Ask students to point out the words with double letters (*ll, pp, nn, ee, bb*). Make sure they recognise that the double letters work together to make one sound.

Help students create alliterative sentences using words that end in short *y* and have double letters.

Jolly Jilly juggled jelly.

Peppy the puppy plopped in the pool.

Happy Holly hogged the honey.

Students can write their sentences and illustrate them.

Point out the exclamation mark at the end of *What a sleepy puppy!* Remind students that exclamations are used to show surprise, a loud voice or a strong emotion.

Ask students to suggest sentences for the double-letter words: *daddy, happy, lolly, hobby, sunny, hurry, wobbly, messy, skinny, muddy, grubby, witty, smelly, cheeky, hilly* and *sleepy*.

Ask students to suggest sentences for words that end in a short *y*: *rusty, dusty, rocky* and *lucky*.

Spelling Focus: Long vowel sounds **a-e**, **e-e**

Student Book 1 **Unit 9**

Label the pictures in question 1 with students, saying each word carefully to discriminate between the long *a* and short *a* sounds. The words are *cat, cape, cake, cap, man, mane, sack, rat, rake.*

Here is the list word that cannot be made in question 3.

Say the list words *ate, cake, bake, take, late, gate, date, game, name* to students. Ask students what sound they hear in each word: the letter *a* saying its own name. Say the words again and ask students to listen for the long *a* sound and repeat the words after you. Write the words on the board and point out the e at the end of each word. Tell students that the e at the end makes the vowel say its own name inside the words. Ask students to suggest rhyming words, for example *sake, rake, lake* and *rate, mate*. Students might suggest words like *ache* and *great*. Include the words, but point out the different spellings.

Write *name* and *game* and ask students for rhyming words, for example *same, came, blame, lame, shame, tame, fame.*

The final list word for students to learn is *here*. Students might suggest it has an *ear* in it, so point out the letter combination for them.

Make sure students realise that the e at the end of each word is silent.

Spelling Focus: Long vowel sounds **i-e**, **o-e**, **u-e**

Student Book 1 **Unit 10**

Have students look at the rude face drawing in question 3. They might enjoy drawing their own rude faces. Discuss the shape of the eyes, the mouth, the tongue, the eyebrows. Have them write *rude* in large letters on the art work.

The list words include vowels *i* and *o* that say their own names inside words. (The exception is that *o* in *hole* does not say its own name.) The words end in a silent e.

The other vowel sound presented in this unit is *u* that says *oo* in *rude*. Other *u*-e words are *flute, mule, brute, tune, compute.*

Encourage students to listen to the sounds in each word and make sure they understand that the silent e on the end affects the sound that the vowel makes. Students should be able to sound out and spell the words.

Students also need to notice that the s in *nose* makes the z sound. Create a list of rhyming words for *nose* to help students remember the z sound, for example *hose, rose*. Students might suggest *toes, goes* and *doze* so make sure you focus their attention on the particular letter combinations.

Write these words on the board and ask students to chop a letter off to make a new word: *hope, hide, toe, smile, fine, hope, ripe, stone, ride, cope, cape, shine, kite, note.*

Spelling Focus: Consonant digraph **ch**; irregular plurals

Student Book 1 **Unit 11**

Some words don't change at all when they become plural, for example *sheep, deer, fish*.

Most of the list words start with *ch*, but three words end in *ch*: *rich, much, such*. These words are spelt the way students will expect to spell them, without any tricky letters or sounds, and so should be straightforward for them to learn.

Chin, chop, chat, chips are spelt with regular letter combinations and short vowels.

The words *child* and *children* should be discussed with students. *Children* will be easier for students to learn to spell, and then they can use analogy to remember how to spell *child*. They could also use the memory trigger of pronouncing the word *child* with a short *i*.

Chase has the *a*-e combination where the e is silent and the *a* makes the long *a* sound, saying its own name inside the word.

Ask students what sound they hear in *here, hear, cheer*. The words rhyme, so they sound the same, but they have different spelling patterns.

Write the words out for students. Point out the differences and have students practise writing all the words to reinforce the spelling. Show students how to use 'look, say, cover, write, check'.

As a mnemonic, students can be reminded that they *hear* with their *ear*.

Tell students to *cheer the deer and reindeer*, to remind them of the *eer* spelling pattern for these words.

Start word banks that show other words with the same spelling patterns. (At this stage in their spelling, students will probably only need the one example of the *ere* spelling provided by the word *here*.)

Students need to know that some words become more than one when you add s, for example *chip/chips, ear/ears, nose/noses*. They also need to learn that some words become plural by changing letters instead of by adding s. Words that change when they become plural include *child/children, man/men, foot/feet, tooth/teeth*.

Spelling Focus: Revision

Student Book 1 **Unit 12**

The word that is left over in question 2 is *family*.

To complete question 3, students need to understand the terminology 'short vowel sound' and 'long vowel sound'.

Revision words include *them, with, those, rude, family, stone, mother, game, smile, father*.

Spelling Focus: Consonant blends **sk**, **sn**, **sp**

Student Book 1
Unit 13

Have students draw the crazy suggestions in question 4. They could draw a dog with black pots on its back, or an illustration for the sentence *If you are hungry, have a snake.* Illustrating these sentences will give a visual demonstration for students of how important it is to spell correctly.

Some of the list words have short vowels: *spin, snap, snack, skip, skin, wasp, desk*. Other list words (*spine, skate, snake*) have the silent e and long vowel sounds.

In *wasp*, the letter *a* says the short *o* sound. Other words with the same vowel sound include *was, swan, wand, want, what.*

Teach students the rhyme *Incy Wincy spider climbed up the water spout. Down came the rain and washed poor Incy out. Out came the sun and dried up all the rain, So Incy Wincy spider climbed up the spout again.* Create spiders with pipe-cleaner legs and display them on a series of painted cardboard cylinders that hang from the ceiling like a drain pipe.

Display the words of the rhyme in the room.

Have students write a story about a snake, a snail or a skeleton using as many *sn* or *sk* words as they can. Publish their stories on a computer. Students can write some of the words they needed to spell for their stories in their personal word books or personal dictionaries.

Spelling Focus: Consonant blends **cl**, **fl**, **pl**

Student Book 1
Unit 14

Make clock faces on paper plates. Children can write the numbers 1–12 on, then use stick pins to attach moveable hands to the clock to learn how to tell the time.

Write the list words on the board or chart paper and say them with students.

Write the following passage on the board and ask students to proofread it with you, to find five mistakes. Ask for a volunteer to read it to the class first, so that students learn that the text needs to make sense to you before you can spell the words in it correctly.

I went to flie a flagg on tope of my flat but the club told mee note to.

Establish the importance of proofreading all writing for spelling errors. Students can use reference materials and refer to their friends as well as you to help them work out how to correct their spelling. Encourage students to read each other's work.

Have students create proofreading passages of their own with errors put in on purpose, and have classmates find and correct the spelling mistakes.

Focus students' attention on the alphabet and the alphabetical order of letters. Students will need to understand alphabetical order to be able to make use of dictionaries in subsequent activities. Students can recite the alphabet as a class, using sad voices, happy voices, sing-song voices, with accents, or as television or movie characters. Some students might also enjoy the challenge of learning to recite the alphabet in languages other than English.

Write the alphabet on the board. Quiz students by covering one of the letters and asking them what letter is covered. Wipe all the letters off the board and ask students what letter comes after *w* or before *k*, for example.

Students can also sort word cards into alphabetical order.

Spelling Focus: Vowel digraph long **oo**

Student Book 1
Unit 15

Write the list words onto cards and ask students to place them in alphabetical order. You'll need to point out to students how to decide which of *school* and *spoon* should come first, and which of *roof* and *room*.

Read the proofreading passage at question 4 to students to help them establish the meaning of the text before they proofread.

Suggest that students write letters to the tooth fairy describing what they will do with the money left by the tooth fairy for teeth that have fallen out.

Dear Tooth Fairy,

This is what I'll do with the money you give me . . .

Have students create picture books. Use the Rod Campbell *Dear Zoo* story as a model. Students can write *Dear Zoo, I need a pet. Please send me one.* The story continues *They sent me a ______. It was too ____________. I sent it back.* To end the story, students are sent a perfect pet that they keep.

Have students write about their school. Encourage students to attempt to spell the words they need. Tell them to get their ideas down in writing first and then check for correct spelling before they publish their writing. Suggest they write about the best and worst things about school, who their friends are, the name of the school and any other ideas they like. Write some key words on the board for student reference. Students can write some of the words they needed to spell in their personal word books or personal dictionaries.

Spelling Focus: Final consonants **s** and **ss**

Student Book 1
Unit 16

Read students 'kissing frogs' stories to maximise the appeal of the drawing at the top of page 36.

Mess, moss, kiss, fuss, dress contain short vowels and the double s.

Plus and *minus* have short vowels but a single s. Students need to become familiar with the visual patterns in these words so that they can tell when the words look right.

In *pass, class* and *grass*, the *a* says *ar* and there is a double s. *Bath* and *path* also contain the *a* that says *ar*.

Have students use their poshest voices to repeat the rhyme *I sat on the grass with my class and said pass the glass.* Have them copy it from the board onto paper in their best handwriting, and read it from their papers to practise. Give students turns to see who sounds the most posh.

Play a memory game with students. Write the ten list words onto cards. Place them in rows face up, in random order.

Tell students to look and memorise all of them. Cover the words with a tea towel or some other cover. Remove one of the words without students seeing which one you are taking away. Ask students which word is missing. Ask students to attempt to spell the word, or have all students recite the spelling as the word is replaced.

Divide the class into groups of three students. Have each group sort out amongst themselves who would be first, second and third if they took turns in alphabetical order. Tell them to stand in a line in alphabetical order using their first names.

Spelling Focus: Consonant blend **nd**

Student Book 1 **Unit 17**

Have students work in pairs or small groups to write stories about a magic wand and three wishes. Suggest that one student in the group acts as scribe while all students contribute ideas and suggestions. Have students collaborate to proofread the stories for correct spelling then read their stories to the class.

The list words focus on short vowels and the *nd* blend. Ask students to suggest rhyming words for all the list words and make up a sentence to say using the word they suggest. Examples are:

end, send, bend, mend, lend, fend
hand, sand, and, stand, grand, band, land, bland
kind, wind (as in *wind up the toy*), *rind, find, mind*
wind (as in *the wind blew*), *pinned, tinned*
pond, blonde, fond, frond

Students have learnt the spelling of *mother* and *father* in a previous unit and so now can create the compound words *grandmother* and *grandfather*. Remind students that compound words are two complete words that join to make one new word. Ask them to suggest some compound words, for example *playground, football*.

Have students clap the syllables and say the words in the list – one clap per word except for *grandmother* and *grandfather*, which contain three syllables each so require three claps.

Play a name game with students to reinforce syllabification. The benefit of recognising syllables is that it helps break words into chunks for spelling. Knowing that syllables must contain a vowel is also useful for working out spelling. Ask students to decide how many syllables there are in their names and create a movement sequence for the number of beats. Some students might like to use first and surnames. They can rehearse and then show the rest of the class their sequence. Students can form groups and join their movement sequences together. They can also chant their names as they make the movements.

Spelling Focus: Revision

Student Book 1 **Unit 18**

Teach students how to complete the word puzzles at question 1 so that they understand that the last letter in each word is the first letter in the next word. Point out the picture clues that will help them choose the correct answers.

Revise the spelling patterns students have learnt about in previous weeks by sorting words into alphabetical order.

Write words on the board (three or four words at a time) and ask students to suggest alphabetical order. Challenge students to work out the alphabetical order for *flap, flat* and *feet*.

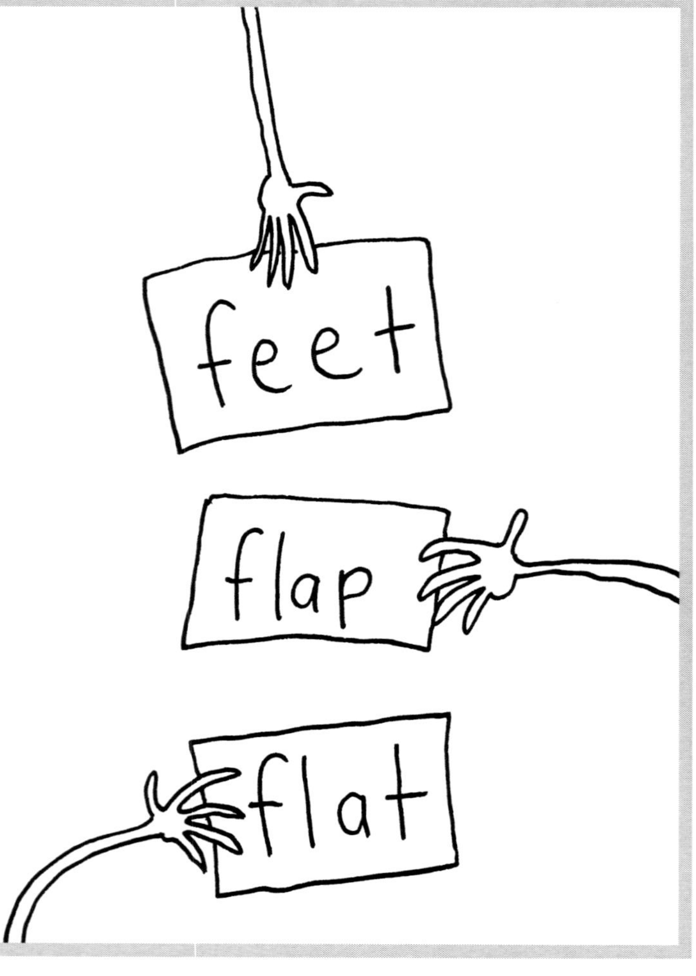

Spelling Focus: Consonant blend **nt;** confusing words **of/off**

Student Book 1
Unit 19

Question 7 asks students to add the suffix *-ed* to the word *hunt*. Explain that adding *-ed* to the end of a word lets everyone know that the activity occurred in the past. Give students examples such as *walked, jumped*.

The list words *ant, went, tent, bent, sent, spent* and *hunt* contain short vowels and the blend *nt*. Have students work in groups to create lists of rhyming words that end in *ant* and *ent*.

The word *want* contains an *a* that makes the *o* sound. Other words with this sound and spelling include *was, swat, swamp, wash* and *wand*. Write this list for students and have them read the words and practise the spellings.

Have students write *aunt* and *uncle*. Point out to students that both words have a *u* and that they need to remember that. Another memory clue can be the sentence *My aunts eat ants. Aunts* is *ants* with a *u* – the *u* that's in *uncle*.

Teach students when to use *a* or *an* in a sentence. Tell them that, usually, they need to use *a* if the next letter in the sentence is a consonant and *an* if the next letter is a vowel.

When trying to help students remember the spelling for *of*, tell students that this *f* thinks it's a *v*. When they pronounce *off*, students should exaggerate the *f* sound so that they remember to write two *f*s.

Spelling Focus: Vowel digraph **ou**

Student Book 1
Unit 20

Make word worms for students to solve by finding the hidden list words, for example *anourloudtcloudnhousemmousefgfound*.

The digraph *ou* consists of two letters making one sound, as in *our, loud, cloud, house, mouse, shout, mouth, found, round, about*. Add to the list as students suggest other words with *ou*, for example *south, count, sound*.

Make a class book and have students contribute ideas for a story about a mouse in the house. Tell students that the first part of the story will tell about the setting for the events in the story (where the house is, who lives there, how the mouse came to be in the house). The main part of the story will tell about what happened, the adventure of the mouse or the people discovering the mouse, or the problem with the mouse in the house. The final part of the story needs to tell what happened in the end. Was the mouse still in the house? Is it good to have a mouse in the house? Was it a happy ending for the mouse?

Write the draft with students, then demonstrate for students how to edit and proofread a story. Publish the story as a class picture book and have students illustrate the pages. Allow them to borrow the book to share with their families. Students can write some of the words they needed to spell for their stories in their personal word books or personal dictionaries.

Spelling Focus: Consonant blends **br**, **cr**, **dr**, **fr**, **gr**, **pr**, **tr**

Student Book 1 **Unit 21**

Make sure that students understand that in question 3 they need to say the word for each drawing, then decide which is the odd one out because it has a different first sound.

The list words in this unit contain various consonant blends, as follows: *tr* in *tree*; *cr* in *crab*; *fr* in *frog*, *from*, *friend*; *pr* in *pram*; *dr* in *drive*; *gr* in *grape*, *green*; *br* in *broom*.

Point out to students particular spelling patterns in the words: *ee* in *tree* and *green*; the long vowels and silent e in *drive* and *grape*; the *oo* in *broom*; and the *ie* in *friend*. Point out to students that *fiend* means a wicked or evil being, so they need to be careful that they spell *friend* correctly. Also tell them to remember that *friend* has *end* at the end.

Students should be able to see when words from their spelling lists or revision words are spelt incorrectly and don't 'look right'. Encourage students to comment when a word doesn't look right and to trust their visual memory for words.

Tell them it is important to really look at words and remember how they look and how they sound, as well as using other tricks for remembering spelling.

Spelling Focus: Digraph **ow**

Student Book 1 **Unit 22**

Question 6 asks students to write the answers when colours are mixed together. It might be useful to include a paint-mixing activity so that students can see what happens when red and yellow are mixed and when blue and orange are mixed.

Say the words in the list to students. Ask them what sound they hear in *owl, cow, how, down* and *brown*. What sound do they hear in *mow, slow, show, grow* and *yellow?*

Write the word *ow* on the board. Have students work in groups of three or four. Ask them to work in their groups to make up a short play that uses words with *ow* (rhyming with *cow*). Tell them that they need to use as many of the words as they can in their plays. Have students rehearse and perform for the class.

Create a collection of compound words on cards and illustrate them, for example *rainbow, eyebrow, snowman*.

Have students work in pairs or in groups of up to four students. Use **Reproducible 8** to make a set of alphabet cards. This deck contains three of each consonant (except for *qu, v, x* and *z*, of which there are two), and five of each vowel. Each student is dealt six cards from the shuffled deck. Taking turns, students attempt to make a word with their cards. They get a point for each card used and replace their used cards with fresh cards off the pack. A variation would be to have students make their words connect to the words of other students in the centre of the group. This is a little more difficult, but gives them access to an extra letter. Students keep playing until all the cards are used or are impossible to use. They add their scores and take a point off for each card they are left with.

Spelling Focus: Consonant digraph **ng**

Student Book 1
Unit 23

Students need to learn about past, present and future tense so that they use the correct forms of verbs in their spelling. Examples are included in question 2: *hung/hang, rang/ring, sings/songs.*

Have students add the suffix *-ing* to as many of the list words as they can (for example, *hanging, banging, stinging, swinging*), and ask them to suggest sentences that use the new words.

All ten list words *(hang, bang, king, bring, thing, song, long, hung, sting* and *swing)* have regular spelling patterns with short vowels, so students should readily learn to spell these words.

Spelling Focus: Revision

Student Book 1
Unit 24

Students need to listen carefully for the first or final sounds in words in questions 1 and 3. Questions 4 and 5 contain cloze activities.

Write the following passages on the board or chart paper, including the spelling mistakes. Have students proofread them and write them correctly on paper or in their books. Read each one aloud to students first.

Miy frend is not a feend. My frend likes to eat grein grayps and crabbs.

I like to see the frogg climb ther twee.

The kinge said bring me the longe fing so I kan banng it and swinge it.

Ther browne couw sat dowun.

Dad said mouw ther grars nowh.

Play alphabet games. Ask students to work in groups of four or five to arrange themselves in a line alphabetically by their first names or last names.

As an extra challenge, you could ask them to arrange themselves alphabetically by the second letter in their first name or the second letter of their last name, and so on.

Spelling Focus: Consonant digraph **nk**

Student Book 1
Unit 25

Question 1 contains a crossword puzzle for students to solve. Explain to students how to use the clues and the numbers to choose the correct answers for each line. Point out that the answers must have the right number of letters to fit in the squares.

Challenge students to create their own crossword puzzles for friends or classmates to solve. Suggest that some students might prefer to work in pairs. This will enable students who are poorer spellers and/or readers and writers to have support. Provide students with one-centimetre grid paper. Allow time for students to solve other students' crosswords. You could photocopy the better ones so that the whole class can work on them, or save them to add to the spelling learning centre activities.

The list words include the consonant digraph *nk* and all have regular spelling patterns using short vowels. Create lists of rhyming words with students for *-ink, -ank* and *-unk*. Make sure students pronounce the words clearly.

Play bingo or another spelling game with the words.

Teach students about past, present and future tense and how this affects spelling. Use *drink/drank* and *sink/sank* as examples and have students use the words in sentences. Ask students to think about yesterday, today and tomorrow. For example:

I drank the milk yesterday.

I am drinking the milk now.

I will drink the milk tomorrow.

The boat sank yesterday.

The boat is sinking now.

The boat will sink tomorrow.

Point out that often if something happened in the past we add *-ed* to it. For example:

I skipped yesterday.

I hopped yesterday.

Spelling Focus: Vowel digraph **ea**, homophones **be/bee**, **sea/see**, **bean/been**, **meat/meet**

Student Book 1
Unit 26

Write on the board the following tongue twister: *Susie sells seashells on the seashore.* Ask students for other words starting with s that could be added into the tongue twister to make it more interesting and descriptive, and also more difficult to say.

__________ *Susie sells* ______________ *seashells on the* ______________ *seashore.*

The *ea* in each of the list words has consistent pronunciation.

Point out to students the word *eat* in *meat*, as a way to remember which *meat* you eat. They can also use this analogy to remember which *bean* you eat. *Eat* contains the letters *ea* and so does *bean*.

Point out the *ear* in *near* and the *each* in *beach* to assist students' memory of the spelling patterns. Create memory triggers for all tricky spelling words. For example:

My <u>ear</u> is <u>near</u> to my face.

We <u>each</u> like the <u>beach</u>.

Have students write Dylan Thomas portraits for the beach. A Dylan Thomas portrait is a poem that asks a question and then uses seven or eight words to answer the question. The answer words are written in pairs.

Have you ever seen the ocean?

Fish-filled, always moving, salty-sandy, blue-green.

If students have never seen a beach, ensure that you provide books and photos. Brainstorm words that can be used to describe the beach and the things you might see, hear or touch there.

Remind students to proofread their poems before publishing them.

Spelling Focus: Digraph **ar**

Student Book 1
Unit 27

Ensure that students understand how to complete the cloze activity in question 3.

You might be able to copy some students' stories and adapt them for cloze activities in the class spelling learning centre.

The list words contain regular spelling patterns that should not cause difficulty for students once they have learnt the *ar* digraph.

Suggest that students write a story about an event on a farm. Brainstorm words that they might like to use in their story and a list of animals found on a farm, and write these on the board or chart paper. Provide factual books and picture books about farms and farm animals. The school's teacher-librarian will be able to recommend a number of stories to read to the class. Students who live on farms or have visited farms might have ideas to share with the class.

Discuss with students the events and activities that can take place on a farm (foxes stealing chickens, lost lambs, floods). Provide time for students to draft their stories, edit each other's stories, proofread for spelling corrections, and then publish and illustrate the stories. Students can then read their stories to the class.

Students can write some of the words they needed for their stories in their personal word books or personal dictionaries.

Play the 'Rhyme Tag' game where students work in pairs and take turns suggesting rhyming words. The first one to run out of rhyming words loses the game.

Spelling Focus: Digraphs **ay**, **oy**; homophones **to/two**, **by/buy**

Student Book 1
Unit 28

Discuss the suffixes that can be added to *play*, *stay* and *enjoy* to indicate past, present or future tense. Ensure that students understand that *-s*, *-ed* or *-ing* at the end of a word can tell you the time of the event.

Students need to learn the sound for *ay* as in *say, play, stay, tray, today, away;* and *oy* as in *boy, enjoy, toy.* Use acronyms to help students remember spelling patterns, for example *boy* – ***b****ig* ***o****n* ***y****owies.*

Point out the spelling of the homophones *to/two* and *by/buy*. Make sure you have a permanent display of homophones, with picture clues. Add to the chart or display any homophones used in students' writing or stories read to the class.

Use **Reproducible 8** to make a set of alphabet cards. This deck contains three of each consonant (except for *qu, v, x* and *z*, of which there are two), and five of each vowel. Each student is dealt six cards from the shuffled deck. Taking turns, students attempt to make a word with their cards. They get a point for each card used and replace their used cards with fresh cards off the pack. A variation is to have students make their words connect to the words of other students in the centre of the group. This is a little more difficult, but gives them access to an extra letter. Students keep playing until all the cards are used or are impossible to use. They add their scores and take a point off for each card they are left with.

Have students play 'Word Webs'. Write a word on the board and ask a student to use a letter from the word to start or finish another. They could also use the letter as part of the middle of the word. You should end up with a crossword-like structure on the blackboard.

Spelling Focus: Digraphs **ir**, **or**

Student Book 1
Unit 29

Onomatopoeia is when words sound like the noise they are describing, for example *squeak, screech, crash, bang, oink, neigh*. Ask your school's teacher-librarian for picture books and big books that use onomatopoeia and share these with students.

Play 'I'm Going to a Farm'. Have students sit in a circle and take turns to say an animal sound using the last sound of the previous word, for example *quack–croak–caw–woof*.

Revise the spelling patterns *or, ee, ea, ir, nd, nt, ng* and *nk* with students.

Add the new compound words in question 5 to the class chart of compound words. Discuss their spelling patterns with students.

The list words contain regular spellings using *ir* and *or*, except for *more*, which uses the silent e.

Write all the words on the board and read them with students. Focus students' attention on the *ir* spelling patterns first, and then later in the week focus on the *or* spelling pattern.

Laminate blank A4 paper and then cut the laminated pages into quarters. Use a whiteboard marker to write the spelling words on the cards. Students can use these cards in pairs to quiz each other's spelling: one student says the word and the other student spells the word. Wipe off the words and re-use the cards.

Spelling Focus: Revision

Student Book 1
Unit 30

Use word cards that have been used for various purposes in the room. Have students work in groups to sort the words using a criterion of their choice (past tense, initial letter, final sound, verbs, number of syllables). Any criterion is acceptable as long as students can show they have used it systematically in their sorting. Or you can choose a criterion for students to use.

Spelling Focus: Numbers **1–10**; homophones **one/won, to/two/too, four/for, eight/ate**

Student Book 1
Unit 31

Use the rhyme in question 1 as a model, but have students rewrite it using rhyming words of their own choice. Have them work in pairs or groups of three. They first need to think up rhyming words for the numbers two, four, six, eight and ten. When they have finished, they can recite their new rhymes to the class. Some students might enjoy the challenge of writing English rhymes for the numbers in other languages, for example *Eins, zwei, catch a fly* (German) or *Ichi ni, climb a tree* (Japanese).

Write sentences on the board that contain the homophones *one/won, to/two/too, four/for* and *eight/ate*. Ask students for their suggestions for sentences.

Play hopscotch. Draw a hopscotch grid in the playground using chalk. Write the number words in the grid. Have students throw a marker into each square in turn and hop through the squares spelling each number word as they land on it.

Write the words for the numbers one to ten on two sets of cards. Have students play games with the cards. They can quiz each other for spelling, or use the cards to play snap or concentration, spelling the word when a pair comes up.

Spelling Focus: Consonant blend **ld**; silent **t**

Student Book 1
Unit 32

Silent *t* is introduced in this unit in the words *often, listen, castle* and *whistle*. Say the words with an exaggerated *t* sound so that students remember that the letter *t* is hidden inside. Point out that *often* and *listen* contain the little word *ten*.

The list words containing *-old* all rhyme and contain regular spelling patterns.

Read the words with students. Point out that if they can remember how to spell *old* then they already know how to spell six of the list words.

The list word *held* also contains a regular spelling pattern. Sound the word out with students. Ask them to suggest rhyming words, write the suggested words on the board and point out any differences in spelling patterns (for example, *weld, yelled*).

When spelling *bald*, students need to remember that the *a* makes the *or* sound. It might be useful as a memory aid to pronounce the word for students using the short *a* sound so that they remember the letter *a* inside it. Another memory trigger could be that *bald* is almost *ball*. Point out to students the four letters in each word and the one letter difference between each word.

Have students work in pairs to write a recipe to grow hair. It could be called *No More Bald!* or any name students decide on. Tell students that recipes include a list of ingredients, and then the sequence of steps, or things that the person following the recipe must do. Brainstorm a list of verbs that students might need in their recipes (*mix, add, pour, mash, tip, stir*). Some of these words could be added to students' personal spelling word books. Have students work with classmates to edit and proofread their recipes and then publish them with illustrations. Display them in the classroom.

Students will need to practise writing and saying *build* and *world*.

Spelling Focus: Vowel digraph **ai**; homophones **stare/stair, sail/sale**

Student Book 1 **Unit 33**

Dramatise *The Three Little Pigs and the Big Bad Wolf.*

Air, hair, stair and *chair* rhyme. *Tail, snail* and *sail* rhyme. *Train, wait* and *said* do not have rhyming words in the list. Ask students to suggest rhyming words for *train* (for example, *gain, pain, rain, brain, chain, remain*) and *wait* (for example, *hate, gate, late*). Point out the different spelling patterns for the rhyming sounds.

Play a concentration game with 24 word cards (12 pairs of words) created on cardboard. Use words from the spelling list for this unit, and include some of the rhyming words. Shuffle the cards and place them face down, in rows, on a table. Have students play in groups of two to four.

Students take turns to turn over two cards. They read and spell the words on the cards. If the cards are a pair, the student keeps them. If they are not a pair, the student turns them face down again and tries to remember where the words are.

While reading big books and picture books to the class, point out the word *said* and the speech marks or inverted commas used in writing to indicate what parts of the story are being said by the characters. Have students read the parts indicated by the speech marks, while you read the narrator's parts.

Write the following on the board and ask students to put speech marks around the words that need them.

Go away, said the green frog.
No, said the yellow frog.

Have students read the parts in the speech marks while you read the narrator's words. If students place the speech marks in the wrong places, read the lines out loud as the punctuation indicates to give students an idea of the function of the speech marks. Encourage students to use speech marks in their own writing. Display a class list of homophone words.

Spelling Focus: Consonant digraph **wh**

Student Book 1 **Unit 34**

Have students work in pairs matched to spelling ability to test each other's spelling knowledge.

Point out the *wh* words that are used to ask questions (*who, why, what, when, where, which*). Choose a pair of students to sit in front of the class. One student asks questions that all commence with a *wh* word. The other student answers the questions without saying 'yes' or 'no'.

Say the words to students. Ask them what sound they hear at the start of each word. All words except for *who* start with the same sound. Have students say the words after you, to notice the *wh* sounds. The words contain spelling patterns that require students' visual memory.

Have students play a game of 'Word Toss'. Tell them to form small groups. They'll need five dice with letters stuck over the numbers. The vowels *a, e, i, o* can be written twice each. Tell students to take turns to roll the dice and make a word with the letters rolled. They get one point for each letter used. For example:

t h n o c – cot, hot, not, no

Spelling Focus: Revision

Student Book 1
Unit 35

Play the game 'Letter by Letter' using revision words such as *nest, slug, baby, bath, hand, roof, house, dress, tent, bird, star, four, world, pink*. Write a word on the board and ask students to change it, letter by letter, until it is a completely different word. For example: *nest–rest–rust–rush–Ruth*.

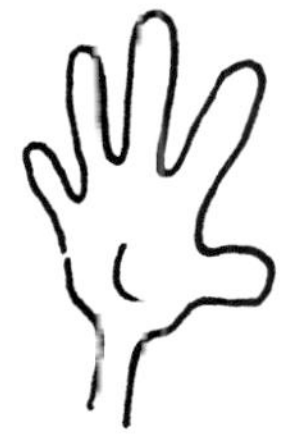

SPELLING RULES!

STUDENT BOOK 2

Student Book 2

Student Book 2 in the *Spelling Rules!* series is designed to introduce students to more complex letter–sound combinations than *Student Books Foundation or 1. Student Book 2* also provides students with further opportunities to expand their core vocabulary of sight words as well as subject-specific vocabulary.

Students are introduced to spelling rules and conventions to help them spell words that cannot be attacked phonetically. They are introduced to the conventions of using prefixes, suffixes and contractions, and develop an understanding of how words are built upon a base word.

Analogy is used consistently. Students are realising the limitations of sounding out a word as a guide to spelling. They are encouraged to apply the rules and conventions to enable them to spell words that are similar to the targeted words and increase their vocabulary.

Students also further develop their visual knowledge of spelling.

Skills Taught in Student Book 2

Phonemic awareness Letter–sound correspondence	Visual knowledge and Kinaesthetic knowledge	Morphemic knowledge	Etymological knowledge
Developing further knowledge of sound–letter representations, spelling patterns and the pronunciation of sounds Developing knowledge of silent letters Developing knowledge of syllabification as a spelling strategy Developing the ability to use rhyme Focusing on substitution of initial, medial and final sounds in words Developing the ability to use mnemonics as memory triggers	Extending on sight vocabulary of high frequency words including subject-specific words Recognising words by the way they look, i.e. their shapes and the patterns made by particular letter combinations Recognising what it feels like to write letter combinations and words Using analogy Using personal or published dictionaries	Using base words with prefixes and suffixes Learning plurals, spelling rules and how changing the spelling of base form of verbs indicates tense Developing further understanding and knowledge of word families linked through meaning Building compound words Exploring homophones Exploring synonyms and antonyms Learning contractions Using analogy Developing knowledge of grammar (noun, verb, adjective) and the effect on spelling of changing words to different parts of speech	Developing further understanding and knowledge of word families linked by place of origin Developing further understanding and knowledge of the origins of words such as food words and students' names

Scope and Sequence: Student Book 2

This scope and sequence chart is based on the requirements of the Australian Curriculum.

Unit	Page	Skill focus					
		Vowels	Consonants	Letter patterns	Morphology	Homophones/ Confusing words	Topic words
1	6	long sounds	digraphs and blends			hole/whole	holidays
2	8				-s, -es, -ed; dropping final e		
3	10				-ed; doubling final consonant		
4	12	short y as vowel sound			-y; doubling final consonant		
5	14		medial ck				
6	16	REVISION					
7	18				-ing; dropping silent e		
8	20				-ing; doubling final consonant		
9	22		lk	silent letters: kn, wr, mb			
10	24	o-e; oa				rode/road/rowed	
11	26	ue		ew			
12	28	REVISION					
13	30				compound words; plural nouns		
14	32				adding -es to words ending in s, x, ss, sh, ch, o		
15	34				irregular plurals	deer/dear	
16	36		st, str			steel/steal	
17	38		tch			witch/which	
18	40	REVISION					
19	42	oi, ai		oy, ay			
20	44	ie, short y		ey			
21	46				adding s to words ending in y; changing y to i		
22	48			aw, oor		draw/drawer, paw/poor/pour, saw/sore, raw/roar	
23	50		spr, scr, spl, thr, shr				seasons of the year
24	52	REVISION					
25	54				contractions	his/he's, they're/their/there	
26	56				-ly; changing y to i		
27	58			er, ir	adjective suffix: adding -er		
28	60			ur, or			
29	62				er, or		occupations
30	64	REVISION					
31	66				abbreviations; suffix -day		days of the week
32	68			igh	adjective suffix: adding -est		
33	70		ld	ould		boulder/bolder	
34	72				compound words: no-, some-, any-, every-		
35	74	REVISION OF UNITS 1–34					

Word Lists: Student Book 2

Unit	Simpler Words	List Words	Extension Words
1	age, plan, ship	hole, nice, time, drive, plane, place, shine, shore, there, holiday	stage, drove, shone
2	thank, love, call	help, stay, wait, rain, like, hope, share, need, seem, finish	stare, chase, change
3	hopped, hugged, pinned	begged, rubbed, patted, spotted, planned, dropped, skipped, stopped, tripped, hummed	chatted, drummed, drooped
4	funny, lucky, messy	lady, pony, sorry, busy, fairy, bossy, foggy, furry, pretty, ready	chilly, woolly, fully
5	back, picked, locked	chicken, bucket, ticket, packet, pocket, jacket, cricket, kicked, pecked, sucked	rocket, shocked, quacked
7	saying, loving, having	going, doing, eating, pushing, reading, riding, coming, making, writing, singing	shaking, storing, repeating
8	sipping, hitting, hopping	running, cutting, sitting, swimming, dropping, shopping, clapping, getting, stepping, beginning	dragging, wrapping, stopping
9	talk, know, write	chalk, stalk, knee, knife, lamb, thumb, wrong, wrist, listen, castle	climb, wreck, soften
10	rope, oats, goal	joke, bone, boat, coat, goat, road, loaf, soap, float, toast	alone, groan, roast
11	drew, stew, clue	new, few, chew, grew, blew, blue, true, glue, threw, knew	crew, dew/due, sew
13	rainbow, classroom, schoolbag	sunhat, gumboot, bedroom, shoelace, toenail, jellyfish, raincoat, hairbrush, newspaper, wheelchair	handshake, toothbrush, doorknob
14	boxes, dishes, kisses	buses, foxes, classes, dresses, wishes, brushes, lunches, branches, potatoes, tomatoes	crashes, beaches, toothbrushes
15	men, rain	fish, deer, sheep, mice, feet, teeth, geese, oxen, children, women	people, grandparents
16	stone, sting, strap	stick, stale, strip, stray, street, string, strong, stripe, steal, stream	stain, strum, steep
17	itch, hatch, pitch	itchy, witch, stitch, catch, hatch, watch, fetch, stretch, hutch, kitchen	clutch, crutch, switch
19	toy, aim, air	enjoy, toyshop, oil, boil, join, spoil, sail, trail, chain, fair	strain, chair, joint

Unit	Simpler Words	List Words	Extension Words
20	pity, jolly, baby	hurry, carry, worry, key, donkey, empty, thief, chief, field, shield	shady, marry, monkey
21	tries, fries	babies, ladies, ponies, jellies, puppies, flies, cries, carries, fairies, hurries	daisies, stories, cherries
22	paw, jaw, raw	saw, draw, claw, straw, crawl, lawn, prawn, poor, door, floor	shawl, drawing, drawer
23	three, scrub	spray, spring, scream, scratch, split, splash, throw, shrink, thread, shrill	thrown, strange, shriek
25	she's, I'd, there	I'll, he's, it's, isn't, can't, don't, doesn't, didn't, won't, we're	they're, wasn't, haven't
26	badly, softly	sadly, loudly, slowly, nicely, rudely, quickly, quietly, crossly, kindly, happily	nearly, luckily, friendly
27	skirt, dirt, day	her, fern, person, girl, bird, shirt, first, dirty, thirsty, birthday	chirp, squirt, swirl
28	or, short, fur	burn, turn, hurt, nurse, burst, word, worm, work, curly, worth	worse, curly, spurt
29	ever, never, driver	flower, river, clever, baker, teacher, doctor, actor, visitor, author, sailor	anchor, cricketer, footballer
31	week, year	Sunday, Monday, Tuesday, Wednesday, Thursday, Friday, Saturday, today, tomorrow, because	daily, yesterday
32	might, tight, bright	high, sigh, thigh, fight, right, night, light, flight, height, weight	tightly, brighten, frighten
33	old, cold, hold	build, world, scold, would, could, should, shoulder, wouldn't, mouldy, boulder	shouldn't, couldn't, elderly
34	someone, nobody, every	no one, nothing, nowhere, somebody, something, anyone, anything, another, everyone, everywhere	anywhere, everybody, anytime

Useful Strategies

In Year 2, students will build on and develop the strategies they use to assist spelling memory. These strategies include:

- building on a core vocabulary of high frequency words that students can use confidently and spell correctly
- focusing on visual differences in words to develop visual knowledge
- using morphemic and etymological knowledge to work out spelling, especially the use of suffixes and homophones
- using analogy when spelling unknown words, especially through the use of rhyme
- using context to determine which spelling pattern is appropriate, especially with homonyms
- using mnemonics provided, or developing their own mnemonics as memory triggers for spelling
- learning to identify words that they can spell and words that they cannot spell, and using classmates, the teacher, charts and posters in the classroom, personal word books, and dictionaries as references
- recording words they need when writing or find interesting in their own reading in the spaces in the student book or in their personal spelling word books or personal dictionaries
- using the list words in their own writing so that spelling becomes embedded in the context of writing
- learning how to proofread and publish written work.

Using *Student Book 2*

Words for the spelling lists have been chosen because of their particular spelling patterns and are not organised around themes or topics, although sometimes a theme might be related through the activities or suggestions in the student book. Most of the list words are expected to be within the vocabulary range of the student. The number of words is kept to ten. This number is large enough to allow students to learn the pattern while ensuring that students are not overwhelmed by having too many words to learn. The activities suggested encourage vocabulary expansion.

Use the list words presented in each unit in *Student Book 2* in short sentences and phrases so that students see and hear the words used in an appropriate context. This reinforces the concept that spelling assists in reading as well as writing.

The student book includes space for students to write their personal spelling words as well as space for students to practise writing the list words.

Each unit in *Student Book 2* begins with a reminder for students to SLLURP. SLLURP is an acronym that summarises the strategies that will help spelling move from working memory to long-term memory. SLLURP also relates to the icons that go with each activity. SLLURP helps to remind students to do the following: **S**ay the word carefully and slowly to yourself, **L**isten to how each part of the word sounds in sequence, **L**ook at the patterns of letters in the word and the shape of the word, **U**nderstand the relevant rules, word meanings and word origins, **R**emember similar words you can already spell and relate this knowledge to the new word, and **P**ractise writing the word until it is firmly fixed in long-term memory.

Assessment

Assess students' knowledge of the digraphs and blends already presented in *Student Book 1* using **Reproducible 16** and **Reproducible 17**. If students are beyond this level use **Reproducible 18** and **Reproducible 19** to assess students' knowledge of the digraphs and blends presented in *Student Book 2*.

Revision opportunities in *Student Book 2* occur at Units 6, 12, 18, 24, 30 and 35. Teachers should identify students who will benefit from revision as well as those who do not require revision but who would benefit from extension activities.

Spelling Focus: Long vowel sounds; consonant digraphs and blends; topic words: holidays; homophones: **hole/whole**

Student Book 2 **Unit 1**

Point out the spelling patterns in the list words and how they are indicated in question 1: *i-e, a-e, o-e.*

Students are asked to find smaller words inside bigger words in question 3. Revise this activity with them first.

Begin to collect on chart paper lists of compound words. Add to the chart as students encounter compound words in their writing and reading.

Begin a chart listing homophones and add *whole* and *hole* to the chart. Discuss the different meanings and spellings of these words, and the fact that they are pronounced the same way.

The first seven list words contain long vowels and silent e. Remind students how to pronounce these words. Read them with students.

Shore is pronounced differently – it has a silent e, but the *o* does not say its name inside the word. Instead, it works with the *r* to make the *or* sound. Focus students' attention on the spelling and pronunciation of *shore*.

Holiday has regular spelling that students should be able to sound out. *There* is a high frequency word that students need to remember how to spell. Make sure they write these more challenging words three times each day and hear them used in sentences to embed the spelling in long-term memory.

Ask students to write a recount about an event or an activity they experienced during the school holidays. Have students proofread each other's writing. When spelling is correct, students can publish their work for illustration and display. Allow time for students to read their work to the rest of the class or to other students in groups.

Spelling Focus: Verb suffixes **-s**, **-es**, **-ed**; dropping final **e**

Student Book 2 **Unit 2**

In question 2, students are asked to add *-ed* to each word that they can. They need opportunities to use the words in sentences. This will enable them to recognise that *I filled the petrol tank* is correct, whereas *I gived mum a present* is not.

The spelling rule at question 5 will also need to be taught (when to add *-es*).

List words *stay, wait* and *rain* include the same vowel sound but spell it differently: *ai/ay*. Ask students to suggest other words with the same vowel sound and create lists for the spellings. This activity encourages students to use analogy. They need to think of other spellings or sounds that are the same and bring that knowledge to the spelling of newly encountered words. Students might suggest *away, day, clay, pay; paint, snail, train, again; they*.

List words *like* and *hope* have the long vowel sound and a silent e.

Share includes the *air* sound, which might also be spelt as follows: *chair*; *questionnaire*; *their*. Create a list of words that rhyme with *share* and point out the different spellings.

Need and *seem* are spelt with a double e.

Teach students the meaning of adding suffixes -s and *-ed* to words. For example *pull, pulls, pulled*. Use these three words in sentences and point out the differences.

She pulled the cart. (This already happened. The event is in the past.)

He pulls the cart. (This is happening now in the present.)

She will pull the cart. (This is going to happen in the future.)

Spelling Focus: Verb suffix **-ed**; doubling final consonant

Student Book 2
Unit 3

Explore with students what happens when e is added to the end of some CVC words: it changes the vowel from short to long, and the e is silent. Use question 1 in the student book to explore the difference e makes to the pronunciation of the words.

In questions 4 and 5, focus student attention on the base words and the double consonant. Ask students to use each word in a sentence, orally. Students could work in pairs or groups of three to write each list word in a sentence to display and read to the class.

Question 6 reinforces the importance of knowing whether a vowel is short or long so that the word can be pronounced correctly.

All list words have short vowel sounds and have either CVC words or CCVC as their base. Write the list words on the board and ask students to tell you the base word for each one. They might be able to underline the base of each word in coloured chalk or whiteboard marker.

Point out the short vowel sound in each word. Ask students to suggest sentences for each base word and then each list word. Ask students what happens to the meaning of the words when *-ed* is added.

Explain to students the spelling rule 'If a word has a short vowel sound, double the last consonant before adding *ed*.'

Have students work in pairs to pre-test each other's spelling of the list words so that students do not waste time learning the spelling of words that they already know.

Spelling Focus: Final consonant **y** as vowel sound; doubling final consonant

Student Book 2
Unit 4

Point out the Spelling Rule! If a word has a short vowel sound, double the last letter before adding *y*.

Have students expand on the lists in question 4 to include words from previous spelling units or words from lists in the classroom.

Students could write the Tooth Fairy's letter to Tony.

Revise with students the letters of the alphabet that are called vowels (*a, e, i, o, u*). Tell students that *y* is usually a consonant, but when it makes a vowel sound it is taking on the role of a vowel in the word. Read all the list words to students. Ask what vowel sounds they hear at the end of each word. They should notice the short *y* sound. Point out that *y* says that sound at the end of each word.

Point out the long vowels in *pony* and *lady*. Articulate each sound in the words for students and show that each sound is spelt by one letter in these words.

Clap out the syllables in the list words. Remind students that syllables relate to the number of beats in a word, and that each syllable must have a vowel in it. In these list words the second syllable is *y*, acting as a vowel. Also point out that most syllables start with a consonant or a consonant sound, so double consonants are usually split up: for example *hap/py, sun/ny*.

Read fairy tales to the class, including fractured fairy tales. Have students innovate on one of the tales and write stories of their own. Provide time for students to talk in pairs about the topic and to discuss ideas for their stories. Remind students to edit and proofread their stories before publication.

Spelling Focus: Consonant digraph **ck** in medial position

Student Book 2
Unit 5

Use the categories from Unit 4, question 4 (*animals, people, feelings* and *weather*) and play a game where students need to think of as many items as they can for each category before their time runs out. You could use an egg-timer, or allow three or five minutes. Students earn a point for each correct word. Check students' spelling, and have them add the incorrect words to their personal spelling books or dictionaries.

Question 7 includes the word *quacked*. Point out the *qu* combination and remind students how important it is for *q* to have its friend *u* next to it.

All the vowels in the list words have short sounds. Pronounce the list words clearly for students so that they hear each sound in the words. Write the words on the board in front of students and pronounce each sound as you write each letter. Point out that the two letters *ck* make one sound in each list word. Ask students which list word has another sound that is made by two letters (*ch* in *chicken*).

Make sure students take note of the words that end in *ed* and those that end in *et*, and the sounds made by the letter combinations. Have students read each word, taking care to articulate the sounds clearly.

Cover the list words and give students a spelling test on the words. Have them correct their own spellings afterwards by looking at the list on the board. Make sure students realise that they now know which words and spelling combinations they need to focus on.

Spelling Focus: Revision

Student Book 2
Unit 6

Word worms have been used in previous *Spelling Rules!* students books but not yet in *Student Book 2*, so ensure students know how to complete them.

Question 2 includes word examples for adding -*s* and -*ed* to words with short vowels that require a doubling of the final consonant (*pat*) before adding *ed*, and words with a final e (*like*) where students need to know that they must drop the final e before adding *ed*.

Revise the spelling rules for adding the suffixes -*s*, -es and -*ed*. Remind students when to double the final consonant. Spend time reminding students about plurals: adding -s or -es, and how spelling sometimes changes inside a word to make a plural (for example, *man/men*).

Revise long and short vowel sounds and words where *y* makes the short *y* vowel sound at the end of words.

Revise the digraphs *ck* and *ch*.

Spelling Focus: Verb suffix **-ing**; dropping silent **e**

Student Book 2
Unit 7

Students need to learn to recognise vowel sounds inside syllables for question 5. For example, they are asked whether *pushing* or *doing* have the same vowel sound in the first syllable as *cooking*.

Teach students how to add *-ing* to base words such as *go, do, eat, sing, push, read*. Students might be able to use analogy to remember the spelling of *read* because the *ea* makes the same vowel sound as in *eat*. They learnt how to spell *eat* in *Student Book 1*.

Students also need to learn how to add *-ing* to words that end in a silent e. They need to learn to drop the final silent e when adding *-ing*. Examples in the list include *riding, making, writing, coming*.

Spelling Focus: Verb suffix **-ing**; doubling final consonant

Student Book 2
Unit 8

Question 6 asks students to group the words according to rules for adding *-ing*. One group would include *shopping, digging, dripping* because they contain short vowels and double the final consonant. Another group would include *doing, singing, sleeping*. The third group includes words that need to drop their final silent e to add *-ing: writing, driving, hiding*.

Revise capital letters and full stops as punctuation marks in students' writing. Point out examples of these punctuation marks as well as question marks and speech marks (inverted commas) in books that you read to the class.

Nine of the list words contain short vowel sounds in their first syllables, which means that the consonant before the *-ing* suffix needs to be doubled. The tenth list word is *beginning*. The short *i* vowel sound in the second syllable means that the final consonant *n* needs to be doubled before adding *-ing*.

Have students circle or underline the base words in the spelling list (*run, cut, sit, swim, drop, shop, clap, get, step* and *begin*). Focus students' attention on the double consonants and make sure they understand why it is necessary to double the final consonant before adding *-ing*.

Point out to students that the list words are all doing words, or verbs. Have students take turns to mime the actions for each verb. You could play a game of charades and have the rest of the class try to guess the verb being mimed.

Spelling Focus: Consonant digraph **lk**; letter patterns with silent letters: **kn**, **wr**, **mb**

Student Book 2
Unit 9

Start a class chart of words with silent letters. As well as list words, include words from the unit and other words as they arise during classroom activities.

Write the list words on the board, reading them to students as you write. Sound out each word slowly as you write and ask students to compare the number of letters in each word with the number of sounds. Write the number of sounds alongside each word. Ask students what they notice about the words: some of the letters join to make one sound (*ch* in *chalk*, *ng* in *wrong* and *th* in *thumb*). Some of the letters are silent (*k* and e in *knife*, *t* in *listen* and *castle*). Tell students that sometimes it helps you to remember the spelling of a word if you pronounce the word incorrectly as you write it down for spelling. Tell them to sound the silent letters in the words as memory triggers and say them all again: *cha-l-k, k-n-ee, lis-ten, lam-b*.

Read them through in this way a number of times so that students use their auditory memory to embed the words in long-term memory.

Have a pre-test. Cover the list words on the board and call out the words one by one for students to write in their spelling test books or on paper. Use the incorrect pronunciation to trigger students' memories. Allow students to correct their own spelling from the words on the board and then swap for checking with a partner.

Discuss students' test results with them. Ask if it helped with spelling to say the words the wrong ways. Help students determine which words they need to focus on learning and which words they already know.

Spelling Focus: Long vowel sound **o-e**; vowel digraph **oa**; homophones: **rode/road/rowed**

Student Book 2
Unit 10

Question 4 involves a crossword puzzle with clues across and down. Check that students understand how to solve crosswords and make sure they realise the correct number of letters must fit in the boxes provided.

List words containing the long vowel and silent e combination are *joke* and *bone*.

All other list words contain *oa*, which makes the long *o* sound in the words. The consonants in the words make regular sounds, so once students recognise the letter combination *oa*, the list words will be relatively easy for students to memorise.

Challenge students to use list words and create word worms for classmates to solve.

Challenge students to write a story that includes as many list words as they can. Remind them to check for correct spelling, and have students read their stories to the class or to groups of classmates.

You might like to publish the stories as a class book.

Provide students with centimetre grid paper and have them use the list words to create findaword puzzles for classmates to solve. You might want to laminate the puzzles for re-use or include them in the class spelling learning centre.

Write and read the homophones *rode, rowed* and *road* for students. Ask students if they remember what a homophone is. Provide students with a sheet of A4 paper each. Tell each student to choose one of the words *road, rode* or *rowed* and write a sentence and illustrate it for a class book. Staple the pages together as a book with a cover and a title. Encourage students to take the book home to read to their families.

Spelling Focus: Digraphs **ew, ue**

Student Book 2
Unit 11

Read the cloze activity in question 7 to the class, leaving the answers out, to help students get an idea of the meaning of the text before they attempt to insert the correct answers.

Read the list words to students and ask what vowel sound they hear in each word. Write the words for them and point out the *ew* and the *ue*. The *ue* words have a long vowel sound *u* and a silent e.

Tell students that there are also other ways to spell the vowel sound, for example in *moon, shoe, you, fruit*. Make a chart for all words that have the *ew* sounds. Write columns of words that have the same spelling patterns on the chart (*ew, ue, u-e, oo, oe, ou, ui*). Write the *ew* sounds in the words in a different colour.

Point out any rhyming words in students' suggestions and make sure students know to use analogy to assist in triggering their memory for spelling patterns.

Blew and *blue* and *new* and *knew* are homophones. Explain their meanings to the class. Ask students to suggest sentences that use the words correctly. Write a sentence for each pair of homophones and ask for student volunteers to illustrate the sentences on art paper. Display the sentences in the room and refer to them regularly so that the spelling patterns are reinforced.

Have students focus on and write three of the list words each day to practise their spelling.

Teach students about opposites. Ask them for examples of opposites. Start with the list words *new, true, few*. Use oral quizzes on opposites as transition activities before lunchtime or moving between activities in the room. Challenging students to think about opposites helps to expand their vocabularies and makes them more aware of the meanings of words.

Spelling Focus: Revision

Student Book 2
Unit 12

Question 2 asks students to determine whether words are verbs or nouns. The word that can be used as both is *glue*. *(Pass the glue. Glue this here.)*

Question 5 answers are *dive, joke, thumb, knew*. Students need to use the initial sound (onset) from the first word and the ending (rime) from the second word.

Review the last five units of list words with the class. Have them clap the syllables for the words. Remind students how to find the syllables and how to determine the number of syllables in a word. An awareness of syllables and an understanding of how they work assists in breaking up words to work out spelling.

Revise verbs with students. Remind students that verbs are things you can do such as *eat, hop, listen*.

Teach students that nouns are names such as the name of a person or a place or a thing. Give students examples of nouns such as *Claire, shoe, cloud, dinner*. Ask students to suggest nouns.

Spelling Focus: Compound words; plural nouns

Student Book 2
Unit 13

Write the words for the numbers one to ten and display them in the classroom.

The list words are all compound words. Revise with students what compound words are. Have students learn three words each day by writing the word a number of times and focusing on the spelling patterns, any phonological knowledge they may need, and the way the word feels as the letters are written. Remind students to think about other words with the same spelling patterns as any of the list words so that analogy will help them remember the spelling patterns.

Spelling Focus: Adding suffix **-es** to words ending in **s, x, ss, sh, ch, o**

Student Book 2
Unit 14

Write the spelling rules for plurals on chart paper or make posters for display:

'Add es to make the plural when the word ends in *s, x, ss, sh* or *ch*.'

'Add es to make the plural when the word ends in an *o* that follows a consonant.'

This unit deals with making plurals by adding -es to words. Write the base words for the list words on the board (*bus, fox, class, dress, wish, brush, lunch, branch, potato, tomato*). All the list words have a short vowel in their first or only syllable. Point out to students that each word is complete and to make it plural all you need to do is add es. Read the plural words to students and ask them to listen for the pronunciation of the -es in each word. In all the words except for *potatoes* and *tomatoes*, the -es is a syllable in itself.

Potato and *tomato* end in *toes* when they become plurals. Draw tomatoes and potatoes with little toes to assist students' visual memory. Point out that *hairbrush* and *lunchbox* (in question 3) are compound words.

Write the list of ordinal numbers from *first* to *tenth* for students. Teach students the ordinal numbers.

Spelling Focus: Irregular plurals; homophones: **deer/dear**

Student Book 2 **Unit 15**

Tell students that some nouns do not change when they become plural. These nouns include list words *fish, sheep* and *deer*. Use the words in sentences for students and make sure you demonstrate one of each animal and then a number of each animal. For example:

The sheep ate its food.

The sheep ate their food.

Write the rest of the list words and alongside them write their singular form (*mouse, foot, tooth, goose, ox, child, woman*).

Questions 2 and 3 ask for singular and plural forms of words such as *ox, foot* and *woman*. Remind students about adding -s and -es to words, or changing the words to make them plural or singular.

Have students play spelling bingo with the list words so that the spelling patterns are reinforced. Distribute copies of the bingo word card on **Reproducible 9**, and tell students to select six words each and copy them onto the card. They must copy the spelling correctly because if any words are wrong they will be disqualified from the game. Have one student call and spell the list words in random order. Players tick off the spelling words they have written as they are called. The first student with six words ticked calls out 'Bingo!', and is the winner. A variation is to have students spell all their words correctly before they can claim to be the winner. Each winner takes their turn calling words to the class.

Point out to students the spelling and pronunciation of the words *deer/dear*. Remind students that these sorts of words are called homophones. Use the words in sentences for students.

Spelling Focus: Consonant blend **st**; consonant cluster **str**; homophones: **steel/steal**

Student Book 2 **Unit 16**

Write the list words on the board. Read them to students. Ask students to look for little words inside any of the list words (for example, *ring* in *string*, *tea* in *steal*).

Ask students what other things they notice about the words and their spelling. Students might suggest the *st* and *str* blends, the long *i* and silent e in *stripe* and so on. Ask them if any of the list words remind them of other words they have learnt (analogy). Discuss the things they notice in the words.

Read the cloze passage, question 4, to students, inserting the word 'blank' in each gap. Assist students to make sense of the passage so that they can choose appropriate words to fill the gaps.

Ask students to work with partners to write stories that use the words *steel* and *steal*. Tell them to use the words as often as possible in their stories while ensuring the story still makes sense. Remind students of the meanings of the homophones.

When the stories are complete, make sure students proofread for correct spelling and then allow time for students to read their stories to classmates. Display the stories or compile them in a class book.

Spelling Focus: Consonant cluster **tch;** homophones: **witch/which**

Student Book 2 **Unit 17**

Write the list words on the board in front of students and say them as you write them. Have students repeat them after you. Ask students to tell you how many sounds there are in each word and write the numbers alongside the words, for example *itchy* (3), *stitch* (4).

Tell students the spelling rule:

'*ch* can begin or end a word; *tch* can never begin a word.'

Have students focus on the placement of the *tch* in the words.

Ask students to suggest words that start with *ch*, for example *chicken, chips, choose*.

Tell them that words ending in *tch* need an *es* to make them plural, for example *stitches*.

Question 4 includes a crossword with across and down clues. Ensure that students remember how to complete this sort of word puzzle.

If appropriate in your school, have students write stories about magic witches.

Students need to know their alphabet to find a word easily in a dictionary. Play alphabet games to reinforce students' knowledge and understanding of alphabetical order. Ask students to arrange themselves in a line, alphabetically by their first names, last names or middle names. Then ask them to arrange themselves alphabetically by the second letter in their first name and the second letter of their last name, and so on.

Ask students to work in pairs to write the list words in alphabetical order. If this is too difficult for your students, choose three to five words for them to place in alphabetical order.

Spelling Focus: Revision

Student Book 2 **Unit 18**

In question 7, the answers are *thumb, wrist, listen, knife*.

Read question 8 to students before they attempt the proofreading. When they have checked for spelling errors, have them swap their work with a partner to ensure students have many opportunities to embed spelling patterns in long-term memory.

Revise plurals with students, and when they need to add -*s* or -*es* to words.

Revise adding -*ed* and -*ing* to words.

Spelling Focus: Digraphs **oy**, **ay**; vowel digraphs **oi**, **ai**

Student Book 2
Unit 19

Ask students to think about the sounds in the words *boy/boil, joy/join, toy/toil, say/sail, ray/rain, way/wait*. Challenge them to try to find other words with the same sounds and examine the spelling patterns.

The spelling list words contain the spelling patterns *oi* and *ai* as well as *oy*. Write the words that have the *oy* sound first: *enjoy, toyshop*. Other list words contain *oi* that says *oy*: *oil, boil, join, spoil*.

Sail, trail and *chain* contain *ai* that says *ay*. Brainstorm with students other words that say *oy* or *ay* (for example, *poison, coil, foil, soil, toilet, voice, joy, soy, boy, destroy* and *afraid, daisy, snail, rain, clay, away, day, birthday*).

Explore the following rule:

'A syllable with *oi* or *ai* must always end in a consonant.'

Spelling Focus: Short **y** sound; digraphs **ey**, **ie**

Student Book 2
Unit 20

List words with *ie* include *thief, chief, shield, field*.

List words ending in the short *y* sound are *hurry, carry, worry, empty*.

Focus students' attention on the spelling patterns in the words. Have students copy the words onto paper and learn them. Remind students that when they practise writing a word they should look at the word, say it, cover it (it may help if they close their eyes and visualise the word while they have it covered), write it down, then check to see if the word looks right.

Write *turkey, donkey, monkey* on the board and say the words for students. Ask students what sounds the vowels in the first syllable make.

Ask students to scramble some of the list words for their friends to unscramble.

The cloze passage in question 6 provides answers for the crossword puzzle. Make sure students know how to solve this kind of puzzle.

Have students create findaword puzzles for their classmates to solve. Provide students with centimetre grid paper. Have them write list words on the paper in a grid pattern, then fill in any extra spaces with random letters. Have students give their puzzle to a classmate to solve.

Tell students to choose one list word and write a story. Their story might be about a thief, a donkey, a chief or a key, for example. Allow students to discuss their story ideas in pairs or small groups if they need to, or want to. Students who have lots of ideas can get straight onto their writing. Allow time for editing, proofreading and publishing the stories. If possible, have students type their stories onto the computer for publishing. Some students might need help with this, so volunteers or peer tutors might be useful.

Spelling Focus: Adding **s** to words ending in **y**; changing **y** to **i**

Student Book 2
Unit 21

Write the base word for each list word that is a noun on the board or chart paper (*baby, lady, pony, jelly, puppy, fairy*. Note that *fly, cry* and *hurry* can also be nouns, but have been used as verbs in this unit. Read the words with students, then ask them to suggest how to make the words plural.

Tell students the spelling rule for the unit is 'When a word ends in a consonant followed by *y*, change *y* to *i*, then add *-es*.' Select student volunteers to take turns to wipe off each *y* ending on the base words and add *ies*. Have students read the plural list words.

Students also need to know the rule for words ending in a vowel followed by a *y*; that is, that in this case they add *-s* only. Examples include *day/ days, key/keys*.

Test students' understanding of the two rules using the following words: *daisy, marry, bully, lolly, monkey, donkey, key, pay, holiday, cherry, trophy*.

Point out to students how to complete question 4 using plural words. Tell them to work in pairs and to read the sentences out loud to make sure their answers sound right, for example: *One fairy flies. Two fairies fly*.

Have students work in pairs to follow the pattern and create other sentences for the list words.

Have students work in pairs to write the list words in alphabetical order.

Have students play 'Word Webs'. Write a word on the board and ask a student to use a letter from the word to start or finish another. They could also use the letter as part of the middle of a word. You should end up with a crossword-like structure on the blackboard.

Spelling Focus: Digraph **aw**; trigraph **oor**; homophones: **draw/drawer, paw/poor/pour, saw/sore, raw/roar**

Student Book 2
Unit 22

List words that contain the spelling pattern *aw* include *saw, draw, claw, straw, crawl, lawn, prawn*. Write the list words for students, say the words with students and point out the spelling patterns. A few of the list words make new words when spelt backwards: *warts, was, ward*. Point this out to students.

List words that contain the *oor* spelling pattern are *poor, door, floor*.

Ask students to suggest different ways of spelling this sound, for example *aw, oor, or, ore, our*. Collect samples for each spelling pattern, for example *yawn, floor, cord, more, four*.

Ask students to find smaller words inside the list words *(lawn/law, prawn/raw, door/do, poor/poo)*.

The unit deals with four sets of homophones: *draw/drawer, paw/poor/pour, saw/sore* and *raw/ roar*. Explain the meanings of the words to the class and ask students to suggest sentences for each word.

Have each student choose one of the homophones and draw or paint a picture to illustrate its meaning. Display students' art work. Alternatively, students could act out improvisations that use the words.

Have students play a 'make-a-word' game. Ask students to play in pairs or groups of up to four people. Use **Reproducible 8** to make a set of alphabet cards. Students are dealt six cards from the shuffled deck and take turns to make a word with their cards. They get a point for each card used and replace their used cards with fresh cards off the pack. At the end, students add their scores and take a point off for each card they are left with.

Spelling Focus: Consonant clusters **spr**, **scr**, **spl**, **thr**, **shr**; topic words: seasons of the year

Student Book 2 **Unit 23**

Have students read and say the list words and examine the spelling patterns. The list words that students might need to concentrate on learning are *scratch, spray, scream, thread* and *throw* because of their letter combinations. The other list words have regular spelling patterns that work phonetically, and students should be able to manage to sound out the words and match the sounds to the correct letters.

Question 5 deals with the seasons and introduces the vocabulary and spelling patterns of the words *spring, summer, autumn, winter*. Use picture books to explore the ideas of four seasons with students, especially with students who live in areas that only have two seasons: wet/dry. Make collage posters for each season, showing activities and clothing appropriate for the weather. Draw pictures as well as using pictures collected from magazines. Students could make a collage using the letters for the titles of each poster. Make lists of descriptive words to accompany each season poster.

Challenge students to use the letters in *splash* to make new words (*pal, has, lash, Alps*). See which student can make the most words. Have students try this challenge with other list words such as *thread* and *scream*.

Provide students with centimetre grid paper and have them write list words in the squares. Tell them to fill in the empty squares with random letters and then have students swap their findaword puzzles with classmates and solve them.

Write the following cloze activity on the board and have students copy it down and fill in the missing words from the list. Remind students to take care when copying words from the board.

I saw the cat _________ up and _________ the boy. I heard a _________ _________ and the boy fell in the pool with a _________. I had to _________ him a float.

(spring, scratch, shrill, scream, splash, throw)

Spelling Focus: Revision

Student Book 2 **Unit 24**

Revise homophones *saw/sore, whole/hole, paw/poor/pour, knew/new, raw/roar*.

Have students play a game of concentration to assist with revision. Choose 12 of the most challenging spelling words from the previous five lists. Make two cards for each word used. Place the cards face down, in rows, on a table. Have students play in groups of two to four.

One student turns over two cards. The student reads and spells the words on the cards. If the cards are a pair, the student keeps them. If they are not a pair, the student turns them face down again and tries to remember the positions of the words for their next turn. The next student takes a turn, trying to find a pair.

The winner is the person with the most pairs when all the pairs have been collected.

Revise with students the suffixes *-s, -es, -ing, -ed*. In question 5, the answers are *monkey, chief, scratch, straw, spoil, shrink, draw*.

Spelling Focus: Contractions; confusing words: **his/he's**; homophones: **they're/their/there**

Student Book 2 **Unit 25**

Write the words *they're/their/there* in sentences for students. Have students write their own sentences for the homophones. Help them to work out mnemonics for these three words.

Write the contractions on the board and read them to students. Tell students that these words are contractions. Explain to them that the meaning of the verb 'contract' is to shorten or squash up. Point out that the apostrophe in a contraction marks the place of a letter or two letters that have been left out. Ask students to tell you which letters have been left out of the words. Write the full words for students to see.

Play a quiz using contractions and opposites:

can/cannot/can't

is/is not/isn't

Spelling Focus: Adding suffix **-ly**; changing **y** to **i**

Student Book 2 **Unit 26**

Write the base word for each list word *(sad, loud, slow, nice, rude, quick, quiet, cross, kind, happy)*. Tell students that when we add *-ly* to a word, the word becomes useful to tell us *how* something happens, such as *slowly*.

Add *-ly* to the first nine base words *(sadly, loudly, slowly, nicely, rudely, quickly, quietly, crossly, kindly)*. The last base word requires extra thinking for spelling: *happy* ends in *y* so the *y* must change to *i* before you add *-ly*.

Revise short and long vowels in the base words so that students can group them in question 4.

Say the following sentences to students. *The child sang sadly. The child sang loudly/slowly/nicely/rudely/quickly/quietly/happily/crossly/kindly*.

Ask student volunteers to sing a nursery rhyme such as *Twinkle, Twinkle, Little Star* in the manner suggested by one of the *-ly* words (adverbs). Allow students time to take turns with singing.

Some students might prefer to sing in small groups with friends. Ensure that students understand that the *-ly* adverbs tell them *how* to sing.

Ask students to use each list word in a sentence of their own. They could do this orally, in groups. Students could also do it in writing, in groups, where one student in each group is the scribe. Their sentences could then be displayed and shared with the class.

Focus students' attention on the pronunciation of the vowels in *quiet*. Write *quit* and *quite* for them to see. Point out the vowels in all three words, and the silent e in *quite*, which means that the *i* is long. Read the words slowly and clearly for students while you point to the vowels. Discuss the meanings of the three words.

Spelling Focus: Digraphs **er, ir**; adjective suffix: adding **-er**

Student Book 2
Unit 27

Write the list words in groups, dividing them into words with *er* and words with *ir*. Read them to students and point out the letters that make the vowel sound in each word. Point out other spelling features of the words: *dirty* and *thirsty* both have *ir* and a *y* at the end; *person* has a *son* in it, and this can be used as a mnemonic to help students remember the spelling.

Ask students to work in pairs and sort the list words into alphabetical order.

Discuss the spelling rule: to compare two things, add *er* to the adjective. For example, *small/smaller*. Tell students the strategies they may need to use to spell these comparing adjectives. For example, they may need to double the last consonant to keep the vowel short (*hot/hotter*); drop the final silent e (*nice/nicer*) or change *y* to *i* (*happy/happier*).

Have students collect examples of adjectives that need each type of spelling pattern.

Have students work in groups of three to develop crossword puzzles for other students in the class to solve. They will need centimetre grid paper so they can work out their answers in a grid pattern, and a dictionary to help create the clues. You might need to model the construction of a crossword puzzle for them first.

Have students write what they would like to do on their next birthday to make it a special day. Provide time for editing, proofreading and publishing students' writing. Make sure students have opportunities to share their writing with others in the class.

Spelling Focus: Digraphs **ur, or**

Student Book 2
Unit 28

Write the *or* and *ur* list words on the board in two columns. Read them with students. Point out spelling features of the words, including the spelling patterns *or* and *ur*, the *y* at the end of *curly* (which has the short *y* sound) and the silent e at the end of *nurse*.

Pre-test students' spelling of the words so that they know which words they need to focus on. Advise them to learn three words each day by writing and reading them, and using 'look, say, cover, write, check'.

Brainstorm other words that have *ur* and *or* spelling patterns, for example *curl, fur, hamburger, purr, purse, world, silkworm*. Have students explore the dictionary to find other words with the er sound (for example, *ir: girl, dirt, shirt, third; er: germ, her, verb, term*).

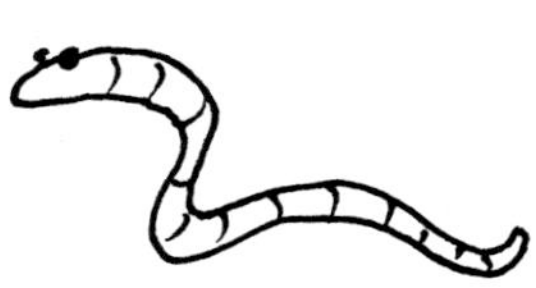

The words in the word worm at question 6 can be categorised into *ur, er, ir* and *or* groups.

Ask students to work in pairs to sort the list words into alphabetical order. Have them choose one of the words to look up in a dictionary so that they can read out the meaning to the class.

Ask students to proofread the following sentences. Read them to students first to establish the context and meaning. You could complete the activity as a whole class or you could choose to have students complete it independently or in groups.

Dad sore the pretti burd land in thu trea. (Dad saw the pretty bird land in the tree.)

Mi sista iz turning ate tuday. (My sister is turning eight today.)

Hiz bruva haz a litl cat corld 'burd'. (His brother has a little cat called 'Bird'.)

Spelling Focus: Digraph **er** at end of word; adding suffixes **-er**, **-or**; topic words: occupations

Student Book 2 **Unit 29**

Tell students the spelling rule 'If a word ends in a silent e, drop the silent e before adding *er*.' Examples are *bake/baker, drive/driver*. See if students can think of any other examples.

Tell students the spelling rule 'If a word has a short vowel followed by one consonant, double the consonant before adding *er*.' Examples are *run/runner, swim/swimmer*. Ask students if they can think of any more examples of people's occupations as per question 3.

Revise the use of full stops and capital letters in sentences for question 5. Six of the list words can be used to label people by occupation. Write them on the board and read them with the class. Brainstorm other words that can be used to label people by occupation or interest. Write the last four list words and read them with students. Point out the *-er* and *-or* endings on the list words.

Have students work individually or in pairs and use dictionaries to look up the meanings for three occupations of their choice from the list that students created when they brainstormed the topic. They can read their findings to the class or to other pairs of students.

Have students work in groups of four to create tongue twisters for an occupation in the word list. Play 'Whispers' with the tongue twisters. Groups give their written tongue twister to the leader of another group. The leader of the group must whisper it to the next player in their group, who whispers it to the next player, and so on until the last person comes back to you and whispers it. Write down what each group ends up with, and read these to all students.

Have students write about what they would like to do or be when they become adults. Have them publish their writing on paper and then compile a class book with a title page, 'When we grow up'. The whole class can be listed as authors.

Spelling Focus: Revision

Student Book 2 **Unit 30**

Revise contractions, compound words, *-er* and *-or* suffixes, and the vowel sound made by *ir* and *ur*.

Create two sets of word cards for all the list words in six of the previous units. You will have 120 word cards. Divide the class into groups of five. Shuffle the cards and share them evenly between the groups. Have students in each group sort the words by a criterion of their choice (past tense, initial letter, final sound, verbs, number of syllables; any criterion is acceptable as long as students can show they have used it systematically in their sorting).

When students have finished sorting their words, ask each group to explain their criterion to the class.

Spelling Focus: Abbreviations; suffix **-day**; topic words: days of the week

Student Book 2 **Unit 31**

Point out and discuss the abbreviations for the names of the days in question 1.

Discuss the prefix *un* with students and point out that when *un* is placed at the beginning of a word it gives the word an opposite meaning; for example *kind/unkind, lucky/unlucky, happy/unhappy, dress/undress*. Ask students to suggest other words that can be given the *un* prefix.

Ensure that students practise and learn the spelling of the days of the week. Focus their attention on particular spelling features of the words, for example the *ue* in *Tuesday*. Mispronounce *Wednesday* as *Wed-nes-day* as a mnemonic trigger.

For question 6, teach students how to use the conjunction *because* to link reasons for opinions.

Start a collection of jokes, word play, riddles and limericks for display in the room. Ask the school's teacher-librarian for a collection of resources. Use the jokes and riddles at the start of each unit in the student book as a starting point for appreciating the humour in word play. Provide opportunities for students to read the jokes and share them with classmates.

Spelling Focus: Trigraph **igh**; adjective suffix: adding **-est**

Student Book 2 **Unit 32**

Write the list words for the class to see, and read them with students. Ask students what they notice about the words in terms of spelling and sounds. Point out the e in *height* and *weight*. Tell students that there is another kind of *wait*, and point out the spelling and meaning differences to the class.

Discuss list words that are similar, such as *high/thigh, fight/flight*, and other aspects of the words that students might notice. Ask students to help you sort out which words in the list rhyme with each other.

Have students practise writing the words using 'look, say, cover, write, check'. Have them test each other's spelling.

Discuss the spelling of comparative adjectives that end in the suffix *-est*. These are used to compare more than two things. For example: *tall/tallest.*

Compile a class height and weight chart. You might like to complete column graphs to display. Be careful not to embarrass any students who might be sensitive about their weight or height. You could use coloured paper streamers to measure head, waist and arm circumferences as well. Expand the unit to include foot and hand prints. Students could create their own personal statistic books.

Have students work in groups of three or four to trace around one student's body, drawing the outline onto chart paper. They could draw on some clothes and paint the body, then label all the body parts for display. Hang the body pictures from the ceiling of the classroom. (If students cut out duplicates for each body, they can staple back and front together and stuff them with rolled-up newspapers to make them 3D.)

Teach students how to sing the songs *Heads, Shoulders, Knees and Toes* and *I'm Being Swallowed by a Boa Constrictor*. Write the words and put them on display.

Spelling Focus: Digraph **ld**; letter pattern **ould**; homophones: **boulder/bolder**

Student Book 2 **Unit 33**

Read the words to students, then tell them to look carefully at the words and read them with you. Tell them to learn three words a day until they have learnt them all. They should practise the words using 'look, say, cover, write, check'. Have students test their friends.

Write the list words in groups according to their pronunciation:

build

world

scold, shoulder, mouldy, boulder

would, could, should, wouldn't

Challenge students to use the letters in *boulder* to make as many smaller words as they can, for example *bold, red, bed, loud, rub, bore, rob, rod, rule, rude, old, do, dole, role, lore, lure*.

Point out the difference in meaning between *boulder* and *bolder*. Use the words in sentences for students. Ask students to each make up a sentence about being bold, and tell it to you.

Make a class book using students' sentences.

Ask students to work with partners and use dictionaries to find out the size of the items on this list: *gravel, boulder, rock, stone, pebble, mountain, cliff*. Have them place the words in order, from the smallest item to the largest.

Have students work in pairs to write the list words in alphabetical order.

Ensure that students understand what they are meant to do for question 1, and that they can distinguish between the different vowel sounds in the list words.

Spelling Focus: Compound words with **no-**, **some-**, **any-**, **every-**

Student Book 2 **Unit 34**

Some students, especially those from language backgrounds other than English, might not be familiar with nursery rhymes such as *Old Mother Hubbard*. Recite the rhyme to students to provide a context for finding *nothing* at all in the cupboard in question 4.

Write the list words on the board or chart paper for students to see. Read the words to students. Ask student volunteers to draw a line between the two words that make up each compound word. Ask students what they notice about the spelling of the sounds they hear in the words. Discuss their suggestions. They may notice, for example, particular spelling features such as the e sound in *any*; that the *o* in *nothing* makes the short *u* sound; that *no/where* looks like *now/here* and so on. Ask students how they will remember the spelling of individual words. Students might suggest memory triggers that are useful to share with the whole class.

Make a set of word cards using the list words, but splitting the compound words into the separate words that make them up (for example, split *somebody* into *some* and *body* and make a separate word card for each). This will give you 20 word cards. Have students work in groups and take turns using the cards to reassemble the compound words.

Point out to students that *no one* is not joined. Ask students to hypothesise about why this is so.

Spelling Focus: Revision

Student Book 2 **Unit 35**

Have students draw their own holiday timetable, based on Ben's timetable in question 5, and write the matching sentences.

Point out and discuss the speech marks (inverted commas) in question 8. Revise the use of speech marks for the whole class.

Review aspects of the spelling covered during the course of the year and, based on students' assessments, determine any areas that need extra teacher focus.

If I Can't Spell a Word...

1. Does the word look right?

2. Do I know other words that sound the same?

3. Can I break the word into parts?

4. Do I know other words that look similar or have the same spelling patterns?

5. What do I know about this word that will help me spell it?

6. Do I know a spelling rule that will help me?

Is the word in my spelling list?

Is the word in my personal dictionary?

Is the word displayed in the classroom?

Do I need to use a dictionary?

Will I ask someone to help me spell the word?

Unit	Dictation
4	Pat the cat.
5	It is a map.
6	I pat the pig.
7	I sit and dig.
8	The dog nips at a cat.
9	The dog sits on a log.
10	The man is sad.
11	The bat is big.
12	Tim has an egg.
13	Pat has ten pets.
14	Dan hit his leg.
15	She has a fan in a bag.
16	The jam is red.
17	Mum is on the bus.

Unit	Dictation
18	Dad has a lot of hats.
19	The pig is big and fat.
20	Do you jog? Yes I do.
21	The fox ran up to the box.
22	Can you fix my net?
23	Why is the sky red?
24	Six eggs are in the box.
25	Sam has many pets.
26	The shoe shop is shut.
27	I wish to have a wash.
28	Tom has six sick ducks.
29	I will jog up the hill to yell.
30	The sun is hot on my neck. I have a hat but it is wet.
31	The three thin dolls are here.
32	The moth is on the path with them both.

Unit	Dictation
1	I pick up a big shell to put in my dish for luck.
2	Look at the queen bee. I can see a good book.
3	Mum can fix the ball. The bull will kick the wall to bits.
4	I can walk fast but if I step in the mud I will slip.
5	Slip, slop, slap and get a hat to go in the sun.
6	I can smell sheep feet. The dog needs a good wash.
7	My father is taller than my mother. I am smaller than my sister.
8	The funny puppy was very sleepy. It sat on the sunny path.
9	Bob will bake a cake to take to his sick brother.
10	Look for slugs under wet stones. They also like to hide in holes.
11	The children like to chase the sheep to the gate.
12	The children smile at the baby. My father chats with my mother.
13	A wasp was resting on a stone. A snake shed its skin.
14	Tim likes to fly his kite. I like to see it in the sky. I clap for the kite.
15	My boot is not in my room. I think I left it at school.
16	The baby fell on the grass in her best dress.
17	My grandmother stands by the pond. Her hat flaps in the wind.
18	My grandfather will get a bus to the pool. He likes to swim.

Unit	Dictation
19	My aunt and uncle will hide. Send my sister to hunt for them.
20	Ben found a mouse in our house. It made Mum shout.
21	My friend has a green tree frog at her house.
22	The owl in the tree is brown. My mum will show my uncle how to mow the grass.
23	The king sits on a swing. He is singing a song as he swings his long legs.
24	My friend lent me a ring. I lost it in the long grass outside our house.
25	I drank a pink drink. Dad sat in the bank and gave Mum a wink.
26	My brother found a shell at the beach. He holds it to his ear to hear the sea.
27	Uncle Chen is a farmer. Mum will park the car in his barn.
28	Max is staying on a farm today. He enjoys playing with his toys in the hay.
29	Pam has torn her shirt. She was playing sport and she fell.
30	It is not dark yet. Can we stay and play in the park?
31	I went to the beach today with my three friends. We found nine shells in the sand.
32	The bald man is building a house. He has sold his old one.
33	Today my family will go by train to see my grandmother. She will wait for us in her car.
34	My grandfather grows wheat on his farm. When I see him I will give him a big hug.
35	I am going to the beach with my friends today. We hope to see a few white whales.

Unit	Dictation
1	I went on a plane for a holiday to the seashore. It was a nice place.
2	We need the rain on the farm. I hope it stays for days. It will help the wheat to grow.
3	The dog begged for chips. I patted it and rubbed its neck. I did not feed it chips.
4	The lady wanted to ride a pony but the fairy was sorry for the pony and said to stop.
5	The chicken pecked at its food in the bucket. It kicked at the mud and picked up a slug.
6	Mum had planned a day at the zoo but our ticket was old. We went to the park and played on the swings.
7	The best things at school are reading, writing and making things.
8	My sister thinks the best things at school are running and swimming. She is beginning to enjoy reading and writing.
9	I listen to Dad singing in the car. He slaps his knee and sings loudly.
10	Dad gave the goat some toast. It bit his thumb. I told Mum the joke.
11	I threw out my old blue shoes. They had holes. I knew my dog liked to chew them. Now I need new shoes or a new dog.
12	My family went on a holiday in a train. We went a long way. The baby got sick and made a mess on Dad's coat.
13	It was raining so I looked for my gumboots and raincoat. I found them in my bedroom.
14	Mum packed our lunches today. Dad is visiting with friends. Mum gave us tomatoes in our lunch boxes. They got squished.
15	The children enjoyed feeding the sheep, geese and oxen on the farm. They saw deer in the forest and fish in the pond.
16	Did you see the fish in the stream? It had blue stripes. I fed it stale toast.
17	Mum found a mouse in the kitchen. She tried to catch it in the rabbit hutch. I wanted to watch but I had to catch a bus for school.
18	The children can all tie shoelaces. They can also stitch up holes in coats.

Unit	Dictation
19	My brother boils potatoes and eats them with toast. I join him sometimes. We wash the dishes when we finish.
20	I worry a thief will take my gold. The field was empty. The donkey had run away.
21	The baby cries when the flies sit on his wrist. His mother carries him away for a bath.
22	I saw a cat catch a mouse with its claws and teeth. I gave the donkey some straw.
23	Do not scream when I splash you or spray you with cold water in the spring.
24	The puppies scratch the floor with their paws. I will make beds for the puppies in boxes with straw.
25	I can't go shopping. I have to fix my bike. I don't know how it broke.
26	One day I was reading quietly on the lawn. My sister told me rudely to move away. She wanted to run on the grass. I crossly told her no.
27	I saw a family singing "Happy Birthday" to a girl. She was too thirsty to eat her cake.
28	Dad got a burn at work. The nurse looked at it. I asked Dad if it hurt but he said it didn't.
29	Our teacher is a clever actor. The visitor stopped at the school.
30	The girl fell and hurt her knee. The doctor and nurse spoke quietly and kindly to her. She won't walk quickly for some time.
31	The best days of the week are Tuesday and Wednesday because I help my uncle feed the ducks on his farm.
32	Tomorrow night I can see the football game. The doctor will check my weight and my height.
33	I stretched my shoulder and had to rest. I wouldn't want to make it worse.
34	Has anybody found my key? I have looked everywhere. I'll have to buy another one.
35	I had fun at school this year. Everyone went to the show. I'm going to see my grandparents in the holidays.

a	a	a	a	a	b	b
b	c	c	c	d	d	d
e	e	e	e	e	f	f
f	g	g	g	h	h	h
i	i	i	i	i	j	j
j	k	k	k	l	l	l
m	m	m	n	n	n	o
o	o	o	o	p	p	p
qu	qu	r	r	r	s	s
s	t	t	t	u	u	u
u	u	v	v	w	w	w
x	x	y	y	y	z	z

Photocopy the letter cards for mini scrabble and other word-making games and activities. See pages 25 and 26 for more information.

BINGO WORD CARD

Photocopy sets of cards and laminate them for re-use. Use wash-off marker pens or whiteboard markers and wipe the cards clean at the end of each unit, or keep sets for revision and consolidation. See page 26 for more information.

Name ____________________ Class ____________________

	Spelling skill	Example/Date	Analysis/Follow-up
Phonological knowledge	Uses recognisable letters to represent sounds		
	Says and writes the beginning and ending sounds of spoken words		
	Uses groups of letters or symbols to represent words		
	Uses phonics to spell words		
	Writes CVC words		
Visual knowledge	Has a core vocabulary of high frequency words		
	Starts to use visual knowledge of how a word 'looks'		
Other strategies	Uses analogy		
	Knows how to use a number of spelling strategies		
	Attempts proofreading		
Attitude	Positive attitude: has a go at spelling words		

SPELLING ASSESSMENT CHECKLIST (STUDENT BOOK 1)

Name ______________________________ **Class** ____________________

	Spelling skill	Example/Date	Analysis/Follow-up
Phonological knowledge	Uses phonics to spell words. Spells CVC and some CVCC words		
	Isolates and writes initial, medial and final sound of a word		
	Spells some words containing vowel digraphs, e.g. *oo, ea*		
	Breaks words into syllables		
Visual knowledge	Can spell a core list of high frequency words		
	Uses visual knowledge of how a word 'looks'		
Morphemic knowledge	Spells simple compound words, e.g. *grandmother*		
	Can build some simple word families		
	Recognises some common simple homophones, e.g. *meat/meet*		
Other strategies	Uses analogy		
	Uses a number of spelling strategies as appropriate		
	Attempts proofreading		
Attitude	Positive attitude: has a go at spelling words		

Name ______________________ Class ______________

	Spelling skill	Example/Date	Analysis/Follow-up
Phonological knowledge	Shows understanding of letter–sound correspondences		
	Spells vowel digraphs, e.g. *oi, ai*		
	Spells consonant blends, e.g. *br, ld*		
	Spells consonant clusters, e.g. *str*		
Visual knowledge	Can spell a growing list of sight words		
	Uses visual knowledge of how a word 'looks'		
Morphemic knowledge	Uses prefixes *un-* and suffixes *-s, -es, -ed, -ing*		
	Starting to use knowledge of word meaning as a spelling strategy		
	Spells contractions, e.g. *don't, I'll*		
	Spells simple compound words		
	Developing ability to build word families		
	Recognises some common simple homophones, e.g *to/two/too*		
Other strategies	Uses analogy		
	Uses a number of spelling strategies simultaneously		
	Proofreads work		
	Uses references (people, charts and displays, personal word book, dictionary)		
Attitude	Positive attitude: has a go at spelling words		

SPELLING CONFERENCE

Name ______________________________ **Date** ____________

1. How do you work out how to spell a word?

____

____

____

2. What is one rule you know that helps you spell a word?

____

____

3. What do you do when you check your writing for spelling?

____

____

4. What would help you learn to spell words?

____

____

____

5. How do you feel when you have to spell new words?

____

____

____

Teacher comments ______________________________

____

____

____

Signature of student ____________________ Signature of teacher ____________________

Z z	H h	X x	D d
L l	B b	W w	A a
V v	Q q	N n	G g
K k	J j	O o	P p
F f	R r	I i	S s
U u	T t	M m	Y y
C c	E e		

Have students name each letter, tell you the sound the letter makes and suggest a word that starts with the letter's sound. Record student responses on **Reproducible 15**. See page 34 for more information.

EARLY PHONETIC STAGE ASSESSMENT – TEACHER SHEET

Name ______________________ **Date** ______________

Letter	Student names letter as ...	Student sounds letter as ...	Student gives example ...	Analysis/Comment
Example *y*	*u*	*short u*	*up*	*Confusing y and u. Needs to focus on differences.*
Aa				
Bb				
Cc				
Dd				
Ee				
Ff				
Gg				
Hh				
Ii				
Jj				
Kk				
Ll				
Mm				
Nn				
Oo				
Pp				
Qq				
Rr				
Ss				
Tt				
Uu				
Vv				
Ww				
Xx				
Yy				
Zz				

Use this sheet to record student responses to the assessment task on **Reproducible 14**. See page 34 for more information.

shop	dash	chop
moon	loud	sea
tail	mother	cow
lick	doll	stop
slip	smell	think
car	play	plan
skin	snap	spell
boy	girl	clap
flop	dress	land
hint	sport	sing
bank	cold	when

Have students read and then spell each word. Record student responses on **Reproducible 17**. See pages 34–35 for more information.

Name ______________________ **Date** ______________

Word	Reads word as . . .	Spells word as . . .	Analysis	Follow-up
shop				
dash				
chop				
moon				
loud				
sea				
tail				
mother				
cow				
lick				
doll				
stop				
slip				
smell				
think				
car				
play				
plan				
skin				
snap				
spell				
boy				
girl				
clap				
flop				
dress				
land				
hint				
sport				
sing				
bank				
cold				
when				

Use this sheet to record student responses to the assessment task on **Reproducible 16**. See pages 34–35 for more information.

walk	knit	wrap
soap	lamb	pest
string	blue	catch
sprig	scream	boil
splash	three	drew
boy	day	key
lawn	door	sail
flower	thirsty	worm
chief	hurt	high
could	build	

Have students read and then spell each word. Record student responses on **Reproducible 19**. See page 35 for more information.

 ASSESSING BLENDS AND DIGRAPHS STUDENT BOOK 2 – TEACHER SHEET

Name ______________________ **Date** ______________

Word	Reads word as . . .	Spells word as . . .	Analysis	Follow-up
walk				
knit				
wrap				
soap				
lamb				
pest				
string				
blue				
catch				
sprig				
scream				
boil				
splash				
three				
drew				
boy				
day				
key				
lawn				
door				
sail				
flower				
thirsty				
worm				
chief				
hurt				
high				
could				
build				

Use this sheet to record student responses to the assessment task on **Reproducible 18**. See page 35 for more information.

My Spelling

I love spelling! I like spelling. I don't mind spelling. I have trouble with spelling.

After each revision unit, colour a face to show how you feel about your spelling work. Share your page with a partner. Discuss your reasons.

Unit 6 Date:______________

How I will do better.

____

____

Unit 12 Date:______________

How I will do better.

____

____

Unit 18 Date:______________

How I will do better.

____

____

Unit 24 Date:______________

How I will do better.

____

____

Unit 30 Date:______________

How I will do better.

____

____

Unit 35 Date:______________

How I will do better.

____

____

My Spelling Assessment

1 What do you like about spelling activities?

____

____

2 Is there anything about spelling that you don't like? What is it?

____

____

3 How do you feel when you need to spell a new word?

____

____

4 What does your teacher think about your spelling?

____

____

5 Rate yourself as a speller. Colour the number of stars you give yourself.
Five stars is the best score.

☆ ☆ ☆ ☆ ☆

6 Finish the sentence.
Spelling is important because ________________________

____

7 If there was one thing about spelling you could wish for, what would it be?

____

____

Use this certificate when you work with a partner to help them with their spelling.

Date: ____________________

Name of speller: ______________________________

Write two things the speller did well.

1 ____

2 ____

Make a suggestion. How can the speller improve?

____

____

Your name: ______________________________

Date: ____________________

Name of speller: ______________________________

Write two things the speller did well.

1 ____

2 ____

Make a suggestion. How can the speller improve?

____

____

Your name: ______________________________

Spelling Rules! Merit Certificate

Name ______________________________

For always having a go at spelling new words.

Signed ______________________ Date ___________

Spelling Rules! Merit Certificate

Name ______________________________

You're a spelling star!

Signed ______________________ Date ___________

Spelling Rules! Teacher Resource Book Foundation–2 (ISBN 978 1 4202 3655 2) © Tanya Gibb/Macmillan Education Australia 2016

Spelling Rules!

Merit Certificate

Name ______________________

For using your brain to think about spelling. Well done!

Signed ______________ Date ________

Spelling Rules!

Merit Certificate

Name ______________________

For proofreading your own work. Well done!

Signed ______________ Date ________

Spelling Rules!

Merit Certificate

Name ______________________

For outstanding progress in spelling. Congratulations!

Signed ______________ Date ________

Spelling Rules!

Merit Certificate

Name ______________________

You're a super speller!

Signed ______________ Date ________

Spelling Rules! Teacher Resource Book Foundation–2 (ISBN 978 1 4202 3655 2) © Tanya Gibb/Macmillan Education Australia 2016

Spelling Rules!

Merit Certificate

Name ______________________

For trying different strategies to spell new words. Well done!

Signed ______________ Date ________

Spelling Rules!

Merit Certificate

Name ______________________

For thinking about the meaning of words. Congratulations!

Signed ______________ Date ________

Spelling Rules!

Merit Certificate

Name ______________________

For excellent effort in proofreading. Well done!

Signed ______________ Date ________

Spelling Rules!

Merit Certificate

Name ______________________

For great achievement in spelling. Congratulations!

Signed ______________ Date ________

Student Book Foundation Answers

Unit 1
1 s; t
2 s; t
3 s; s; t; t
4 s = snake, scissors, slide; t = table, tree, ten

Unit 2
1 a; p
2 a; p; p; a; a; p
3 a; p; p; a
4 a; p

Unit 3
1 s; s; s; t; t; t; p; p; p
2 dress = s; rabbit = t; cap = p; map = p; rocket = t
3 a; a; a; a
4 cap; tap; rat

Unit 4
1 c; g
2 c; c; c; c; g; g; g; g
3 girl; goat; glue; glove
4 cat; cap; gap

Unit 5
1 m; i; m; i
2 i
3 in/is; a; mat; it; in/is; map/sip
4 map; mat

Unit 6
1 m; m; g; g
2 m; g; g; g; m
3 m = circle; m = box; g = box; g = circle
4 am; pig, sits, mat; sit, tip

Unit 7
1 red = drum; duck; dog; blue = leaf; lamp; lion
2 dig; lips
3 pig + dig; tip + sip
4 dig, pig; lip, sip, tip
5 dip, dig; sit, sip
6 lip; sat; tip; pat; it; dad (Answers may vary.)

Unit 8
1 o; n; o; n
3 nap/nip; no/as/on; no/as/on
4 as, am; nip, nap
5 mats; friends; cups; rats

Unit 9
1 l; n; d; n; d; l
2 not/got/dot; pod; so
3 nod, not; dot, dog
4 not, dog; not, pot, on; not, sit, log

Unit 10
1 pin; l; sad; lid/dad
2 sad; pin; dad
3 Students write *can* for answers that apply to them.
5 a; i; a; i; o; o

Unit 11
2 b; r; b
3 rod; bin; rip; rag
5 rat
6 pig: b g, dig; mat: rat, bat: rag: bag, tag (Answers may vary.)

Unit 12
1 circle = egg, elephant, elbow; box = house, hat, hand
2 has, had; hit, hot
3 an; a; an; a; an; a
4 h; e; h
5 hot; hat; has; egg; me/us

Unit 13
1 crab = box; bus = circle; web = box; bike = circle
2 ten; get, pet; rib; bed, red
3 my; get/pet; by; him/ten
4 get, bed; ten, my; pet
5 10

Unit 14
1 net; hit; top
2 bed, bad; hid, had; hot, hit, hat
3 p, s, p, p – cross out sock; l, l, l, f – cross out foot
4 s; b; m
5 his; her; new
6 bad; top; her; new

Unit 15
2 fan; fin; one; fit
3 one, fat; fin; up
4 he, us; she, or
5 up; cat

Unit 16
1 j = jam, jigsaw, jump
2 k = kite, key, kangaroo, kettle
3 jam; jog; job
4 We, the; the, to
5 k; j; j
6 be and we; so and go

Unit 17
1 f; f; f
2 u
4 run; mum; hug; sun/run/fun
5 of; of
6 put, if; bus, if

Unit 18

1 bag, beg, big, bug; bat, bet, bit, but; jog, jug; fed, fad
2 mad; leg
3 j; l; s
4 g; d; t
5 said, you; you
6 but; if; and

Unit 19

1 cat, cot, cut; beg, big, bug
2 pat/pal/pan/pad; his/him/hit/hid/hip
3 fan/man/pan/ran/tan/van; cot/dot/got/hot/jot/lot/not/pot/rot
4 net; bet; get; bed; red; bad; bat; rat; not; nod; rod; rot; god; got; but; nut; bud; gut; rut
5 his; him; for; out; get

Unit 20

1 queen/quack; van/violin; window/wig; yo-yo/yawn; zebra/zip
2 zoo; van; an; ant; no; of; we; wet; to; toy; yes; was; as
3 z; y
4 and 5 Answers will vary.
6 wet; was

Unit 21

1 box; fix; mix; fox; six
2 go; went
3 mix, fix, six; box, fox
4 six; box; fix; mix; wax; very

Unit 22

2 b, e, h, k, p, s, v, x; A, D, G, J, M, O, Q, R, U, W, Z
3 c; i; o; w
4 Answers will vary.
5 a; z

Unit 23

1 fry/try/boy; this; fry/try/boy; cry
2 try; cry; sky
3 Why
4 sky; fly; fry
5 Try; cry; fly; boy, that

Unit 24

1 pigs; hats; legs; ants
2 bag; bats; hens; rug
3 I see six eggs.
4 many; lots; many
5 many, two eggs; How, five cats; How many; six cups
6 Answers will vary.

Unit 25

1 hop; jog; van
2 fix, six, mix; net, not, nut; but, bun, bus
3 dig; cry; fat; web
4 van; ten; mum
5 my; she; he; an; and; the; them; many; any; an; is
6 jugs; cups; eggs

Unit 26

1 shy; ship/shop; now; shoe
3 shed; shy; shop; shut
4 shed; shoes; ship; shut
5 hip; hop; she/he; hut

Unit 27

1 Colour brush and fish
2 wish, fish; wash, cash; push, rush
3 Answers will vary.
4 want; push; your; wish
6 Answers will vary.

Unit 28

1 Colour stick; brick; sock
2 tick, tock, tick, tock, tick, tock
3 u; e; o
4 rock, shock, lock; back, pack, sack
5 sick; does; socks
6 what; ticks
7 was; were

Unit 29

1 shell; doll; hill
2 shall; yell
3 call/well; hill/doll/bell/fell; yell
4 dell; hill
5 Answers will vary.

Unit 30

1 left; right; right
2 o; a; i; u; e
3 let, get, wet; lick, lock, luck; wish, will, wig
4 ill; is; hut; bat/at
5 dog/bog/fog/hog/jog/leg/lot/lob/lop; bell/fell/sell/tell/will/wall/welt; she/sly/spy/sty/why
6 pig; cat; dog; duck; back; neck; lips; legs

Unit 31

1 sh; th; sh; th; ch
2 He; They; She; They
3 Then; When; them; three; four
4 They went to the pet shop,
Can you see them in there?
Here they are!
5 that; then; this; there; thin; this

Unit 32

1 3; 1; 1; 3; 2
2 bath; moth; both; path; with; tooth
3 with; good; some; some
4 bath; moth; path
5 both; good; some; there
6 Answers will vary.

Student Book 1 Answers

Unit 1
1 ship; shop; dish/wish; fill; shell
2 hop/shop; shell; pack; dish/wish
3 fill; shell; pack
4 a: quack, back; i: lick; sick; u: suck, luck
5 neck; tick; duck; sock; sack
6 quack; wish; fell
7 Answers will vary.

Unit 2
1 hook; wool; queen; cook; Peep, sheep, look; see, bee, foot
2 took; cook; hook; shook
3 Across: sheep; bee; foot; look
Down: feet; wool; good; book; see; queen
4 wool; took; meet (Sentences will vary.)
5 need; bee; beef; feed; keep; deep

Unit 3
1 wall; fall; all
2 ball; Pull
3 a, all, ball; I, ill, fill; a, all, tall
4 **a** as in cat: ant, lap, shall
a as in ball: walk, call, hall
u as in cup: gull, dug, dull
u as in pull: full, bull, wool
5 shook; call; pick; look
6 Answers will vary.

Unit 4
1 stop, step, stick; rest, best; fast, last; list; lost; must
2 box; circle; circle, box
3 test; fast/fist; past/post/pest; best/bust; mast/mist/must; rest/rust
4 top/to; us; is; as
5 stick; rest; fast; last
6 best; lost; Stop; step

Unit 5
1 Slip; Slop; Slap; asleep
2 slip; slid; slap
3 slap; slip/slid/slim; slop; slid; sleep; small
4 sm; sl; sl
6 smell; asleep; slip; Slugs
7 Sentences will vary.

Unit 6
1 slip
2 Answers will vary. For example: chop/ship/shot; wash/dish/fish/wisp; tick/pick/sick/wick/lock/luck; sell/well/fell/tell/bill/ball/belt; step/slop; last/lost/fist/mist/lisp; slap/slip/plop/slow/slot/slob/slog; spell/swell/small/smelt; bee/fee/pee/wee/she/sea/set/sew; good/wood/hoot/hoop
3 toyshop; beehive; football; footpath
4 book; nest; bull; foot; wall; bee; wool; sheep; hoof; boot; step; slug

Unit 7
1 mother; father; brother; sister; baby; family
brother; sister; mother
Tareq; father; Reem; mother
2 mother; father; brother; sister
3 computer; flower; spider
4 spider = 2; ball = 1; computer = 3; baby = 2; wool = 1; flower = 2
5 smaller; taller; **er** compares one object or person to another

Unit 8
1 jelly; wobbly; funny; sleepy; puppy; sunny; silly; happy
2 very; body; sleepy; dusty; sticky
3 daddy; lolly; sunny; wobbly; happy; hobby; hurry; sloppy
4 My puppy is very muddy.
Is your tooth wobbly?
Red jelly is so yummy.
5 rusty; sleepy; dusty; lucky; messy; smelly; rocky; cheeky; hilly
6 *thin* does not start with **s**
shy only has one syllable and has a long **y** sound
body does not have a double letter at the syllable junction

Unit 9
1 cape; cake; mane; rake
2 cake; game; ate
3 ate; cake; bake; take; late; gate; date; game; name
Word that cannot be made: here
4 at; hate; mat
5 make, wake, fake, lake; came, same, tame, name
6 ate; game; came; same; late; ate; shake

Unit 10
1 hide, slide; fine, shine; nose, rose; stone, cone; like, bike; hole, mole; hope, rope; toe, hoe; smile, file
2 Cross out: to; hope; not; kit
3 rice; smile; rope; hose; rude; tune
4 I, ice, mice; on; one; stone (Sentences will vary.)
5 hope; hid; like; not; ripe

Unit 11
1 sh: shark, shell, shoe, shadow; ch: chain, cheese, chicken, chips, chair, chocolate
2 chips; chin; shops
3 box; circle; both; circle
4 books; children; feet; noses; men; sheep
5 rich; chat; much; chase; chases; such; child

Unit 12
a, e, i, o, u
2 **th**: them, with, mother, father; silent **e**: rude, stone, game, smile; both: those
Word left over is *family*
3 Short vowel sound: met, fuss, at, slid
Long vowel sound: ate, toe, these, cape, slope
4 same, lame, tame; rose, hose, nose
5 chase; sunny; hide; sleepy

Unit 13
1 sn; sk; sp; sn; sk; sp; sn; sp, sn; sp
2 spin, spine, wasp; snack, snake, snack; skip, skin, desk
3 Across: skin, skip, spin, wasp, skate
Down: spine, snake, spade, snack
4 spin; snack; spot
5 as/ask; ill/kill; spin/in/pin/pine; as/was/asp
6 snack; spot; skin

Unit 14

1 cl; fl; pl; cl; fl; cl; fl; pl
2 fly; plan; clap, place
3 plum, plug, plant; clap, clip, class; slug, slip, slide; flip, flop
4 plate, play; clock, clap; flag, flaps

Unit 15

1 pool; zoo; boot/food; moon/room; roof; spoon, school, tooth
2 **oo** as in took: book, hook, foot; **oo** as in food: broom, moon, boot, tooth, stool
3 bedroom; bathroom; classroom
Other answers will vary.
4 look; boots; cake; spoon; pool; gone

Unit 16

1 grass; Class, DRESS
2 mess/dress; kiss; moss; fuss/plus/minus; mess/dress
3 tick; cross; plus; minus
4 moss; fuss; pass; dress
5 hiss; toss; mess; class; lass; kiss; pass
6 Answers will vary.

Unit 17

1 sand; hand; band; wand; land
Circle: wand
2 send; pond; end; wind; sand; kind/wind
3 mother = 2, stand = 1, sand = 1; grandmother = 3, hand = 1; grandfather = 3, stands = 1, water = 2; fishing = 2
4 and; grandfather; on; kind; bend; windy
5 First sentence: wind = green
Second sentence: wind = blue

Unit 18

1 roof, feet, meet, room; flap, play, they, flat
snap, pool, tool, spot; book, kiss, eyes, bike
2 skin; moon; kind; flat
3 clock; food; miss; plate
4 likes; club, school, spends, classroom

Unit 19

1 tent: ant, sent, spent, bent; pond: and, send, spend, bend
2 spent; sent
3 wind; and; went; find; sent; kind; want; tent; bent; mend; sand; bend; land; hunt; found; and; pant; plant
4 a, e, i, o, u
5 an; a; an; an
6 of; off
7 hunted (Sentences will vary.)

Unit 20

1 Answers may include: cloud; loud; mouth; south; mount; count; mound; round; sound; lout; shout; sour
2 a + bout; a + loud; a + round
3 I found a mouse.
We live in a round house.
4 Cross out: shout; add: cloud
Cross out: south; add: found/round
5 se: house, mouse; th: south, mouth; t: out, about; nt: mount, count

Unit 21

1 p; f; b; p; c; b; d; f; t; c
2 crab; tree (Sentences will vary.)
3 cross out duck; cross out grass
4 grab, grub, greet, green, grape, grand; tree, trap, trip, track, trot, truck
5 drive; truck; broom; brick; grass

Unit 22

1 brown: owl, cow, how, down; yellow: mow, slow, show, grow
2 snowman; rainbow; eyebrow
3 clown, crown, frown, town; tow, low, row; how, now, vow
4 low; row; how; own
5 mow; owl
6 yellow; brown

Unit 23

1 hang; bring; song; swing; sting; thing
2 hang; rang; sings
3 playing; growing; ringing; going; spelling; bringing; stinging; swinging
4 Answers will vary.
5 something; nothing; anything; everything

Unit 24

1 tent; wing; wind; bend; swing; plant
2 down; mouth; round; blow; cloud; clown
3 crab; friends; grass; pram; drip; broom
4 hung; went; sang; blew
5 showed; hunted; shouted
6 down; flat; long; found; slow; loud

Unit 25

1 bank; skunk; wink; pink; sink
Hidden word: bunks
2 thank; sank; drink
3 blank; plank; slink; trunk
4 bank; drank; ink; junk; pink
5 drink/brink/shrink; plank; thank; think; blink; bran/rank

Unit 26

1 ear → hear; eye → see; nose → smell; mouth → taste; hand → feel
2 clean; leaf; beach; meat; near; bean
3 near, fear, dear; mean, bean, clean; meat, beat, seat; beach, teach, peach
4 seagull, seashell; seaweed, seashore
5 bee; beans; meets; sea

Unit 27

1 car, jar, bar, tar, far; shark, bark, mark, dark, park
2 car; star/art/tart; bar/ark; arm; bar; car/art; farm/arm; art/he/hear; her/at/fat
3 farm; dark; barn; yard; hard; far
4 father, sheep; any, heart
5 farmer; bark (Sentences will vary.)

Unit 28

1 tray; boy/toy/buy; away; today; play/stay; say; enjoy
2 lay; ray; may; way; day; hay
3 plays, played, playing; played
stays, stayed, staying; staying
enjoys, enjoyed, enjoying; enjoys
annoys, annoyed, annoying; annoying
4 two; buy; to; by
5 today = 2; yesterday = 3; holiday = 3

Unit 29

1 bird; fork; cork; shirt; girl; corn; thorn; stir
2 fork; short/sport; torn; dirt/shirt; bird; more
3 sport; shirt; skirt
4 Sentences will vary.
5 ladybird, girlfriend, anymore, stir-fry
stir-fry; ladybird; girlfriend; anymore

Unit 30

1 hard; stay; start; dark; clean; buy; near; girl
2 Answers may include: neat/seat/treat/beat/heat/meat; bark/mark/dark; dirt; born/horn/torn/worn/shorn/thorn; bay/day/gay/lay/may/pay/ray/say/way; soy/toy; how/cow/bow/row/sow/vow
3 enjoy; playing; card; annoyed; smart; clay; tray
4 cow; sheep; duck; pig; mouse
5 leaf; bee; shirt; fork
6 wink; wind; king; tent
7 star; beach; candle; swing; ear; meat; bird
Hidden word: seaweed

Unit 31

1 one; two; three; four; five; six; seven; eight; nine; ten
2 four; three; one; six; eight; ten; two; five; nine
3 Across: ten; six; four; one; eight; nine; Down: two; seven; five; three
4 one; four; eight; two
5 to; for; won; too; two; one

Unit 32

1 fold; gold; hold; cold; told; bold
2 bad; word
3 bald; hold; built
4 Sentences will vary.
5 build; wood; held; hammer; often; too

Unit 33

1 tail, nail, sail, rail, jail; hair; fair; chair; pair; stair
2 train, rain; snail, nail; chair, hair/air
3 raincoat; fingernail; hairbrush (Sentences will vary.)
4 straw, said; wood, said; sticks, said
5 stair; stare; sale, sail

Unit 34

1 hen, he; hat, at; heel, he, eel; here, her, he; heat, eat, at, he; it, hit
2 wish, went, wind; wheel, white, whale
3 Why; When; What; Where; Which
4 who; why; whale; what
5 Answers will vary.

Unit 35

1 luck; book; walk; stick; slug; bath; puppy; baby; cake; smile; chips; snake; flag; roof; dress; hand; tent; house; tree; owl; king; wink; leaf; star; tray; bird; four; world; tail; whale

Student Book 2 Answers

Unit 1

1 i-e: nice, time, drive, shine; a-e: plane, place; o-e: hole, shore
2 cap, cape; mat, mate; pin, pine; cut, cute
3 place: ace, lace; plane: plan, lane, an; there: the, he, her, here
4 driveway; seashore/seaplane; sunshine
5 List words: hole, plane, drive, there (Extra words will vary.)
6 whole; hole; hole; whole
7 Sentences will vary.

Unit 2

1 helps, helped; stays, stayed; waits, waited; rains, rained; needs, needed; seems, seemed; calls, called
2 Words to be crossed out: run, give
3 kissed: 1; helped: 1; waited: 2; started: 2; needed: 2; asked: 1; jumped: 1; minded: 2; missed: 1; painted: 2; pulled: 1; pushed: 1
4 rained; needs
5 smashes, smashed; munches; munched; finishes, finished; reaches, reached
6 hoped; shared; cured

Unit 3

1 a, mad, made; e, pet, Pete; i, slid, slide; o, hop, hope; u, hug, huge
2 Pics to be circled: drink; swim; skip; hop
3 patted; skipped; planned; rubbed; dripped; chopped
4 begged; rubbed; spotted; planned; patted; stopped; skipped; hummed
5 stopped; tripped; begged; dropped; skipped; rubbed; slipped; trapped; stepped
6 hoped; pinned; planned; tapped
7 Sentences will vary.

Unit 4

1 Words to be circled: crazy; daisy; busy; pretty
2 muddy; sunny; furry/fury; baggy; sloppy
3 sorry; furry; bossy; fairy; foggy; pony
The words *hurry* and *furry* do not rhyme.
4 Animals pony; People: lady; Feelings: sorry; Weather: foggy (Other words will vary.)
5 Words to be circled: wobly; heppy; not; Fary; sory; rubed.
Correct spelling: wobbly; happy; note; Fairy; sorry; rubbed
6 Answers will vary.

Unit 5

1 locked; picked; clicked; packed; quacked; cracked
2 bucket/ticket/kicked; cricket; sucked; packet/pocket/jacket; chicken
3 sucked: 1; bucket: 2; jacket: 2; pecked: 1; checked 1: packet: 2
4 checked – pecked; rocket – pocket; picked – kicked; wicket – cricket
5 a: packet, jacket; i: chicken, ticket, cricket, kicked; u: bucket, sucked
6 packed – packet – pocket – socket; locked – licked – ticked – ticket; packet – packed – picked – kicked
7 sucked; licked; quacked; pecked; kicked; shocked

Unit 6

1 need; needs; so; sorry; the; he; her; here; there; rest; stop; top; stopped; topped; drip; rip; dripped; ripped
2 asks, asked; pats, patted; likes, liked
washes, washed; shares, shared; drops, dropped
3 kicked: 1; happy: 2; place: 1; begged: 1; needed: 2; finished: 2; pocket: 2; drive: 1; windy: 2
4 plane – lady – rain; ticket – cricket; spotty – bossy; drive – time – shine
5 three jackets; two planes; four buckets
6 see; read; pack; in/fin/finish/she/shed; air/airy/fair; bus; lid/day; car
7 barked; mooed; quacked; pony; hummed (Sentences will vary.)
8 Word to be circled: droped; Correct spelling: dropped
Word to be circled: reddy; Correct spelling: ready

Unit 7

1 going; asking; looking; pushing; singing; coming; having; making; writing
2 reading; writing
3 pushing; coming
4 writing; eating
5 eating; going; pushing; making
6 We will be driving to the beach this holiday.
We are making a yummy cake on Mother's Day.
Ling fell when she was riding a pony.

Unit 8

1 running; cutting; dropping; clapping; getting; stepping
2 Words to be circled: rub; plan; spot; trip; chop
3 sitting; shopping; swimming
4 slipping, tripping/slimming, trimming; winning, grinning; batting, chatting; chopping, stopping
5 running; shopping; sitting
6 doing, singing, sleeping; writing, driving, hiding; stopping, digging, dripping
7 Answers will vary.

Unit 9

1 talk; walk; chalk; stalk
2 Pics to be circled: ball; fork; claw
3 knee: k; lamb: b; wrist: w; listen: t; knot: k
4 wrong, wrist; knee, knife; lamb, thumb; listen, castle
5 knife, knot, knock; wrong, wrist, wreck; thumb, comb, crumb
6 2-letter words: no, is, do, of; 3-letter words: now, ten; 4-letter words: know, talk, knee, need, numb; 5-letter words: knock, wrist, stalk, often
7 knelt, listen, lamb; knob, castle, wrong

Unit 10

1 Pics to be circled: goat; rope; ruler; smoke
2 road; bone; coat; soap
3 load, loaf, loan; coast, roast, boast
4 Across: boat, soap, float, bone
Down: toast, loaf, joke
5 toad; cloak; foal; croak
6 soaked; floated; toasted; joked
7 rode, rowed; road

Unit 11

1 flew, chew, grew, knew; blue, true, glue, clue
2 new; blue; threw
3 Words to be crossed out: book; toe; four
4 two; you; shoe; few/new; glue/blue
5 flew; drew, threw; grow
6 chewed; glued
7 Homophones: new/knew; blew/blue
To complete the story: new; blue; blew; knew
8 few; new; true

Unit 12

1 One-syllable words: knife, grew, help; Three-syllable words: beginning; Two-syllables words: pocket, pony, reading
2 Noun only: fairy, wrist, car; Noun or verb: glue; Verb only: blew, get, listen
3 needed, needing; talked, talking; joked, joking; dropped, dropping
4 Words to be circled: swiming; tickits; suny; rane; hom
Correct spelling: swimming; tickets; sunny; rain; home
5 drive; joke; thumb; knew
6 Answers will vary.

Unit 13

1 sunhat; hairbrush; shoelace; raincoat
2 star/fish; school/bag; ear/ring; toe/nail; arm/chair; tooth/brush
3 rainhat, rainbow, raindrop; sunshine, sunrise, sunset
4 Answers will vary.
5 armpit; jawbone; fingernail; earlobe; ribcage; bellybutton
6 two shoelaces; three newspapers

Unit 14

1 buses; foxes; classes; wishes; benches
2 boxes; buses; kisses; toothbrushes; branches
3 socks; hairbrushes; dresses; lunchboxes; shirts; branches; churches; texts
4 tomatoes; volcanoes
5 lunches; tomatoes; potatoes
6 Answers will vary.

Unit 15

1 fish; deer; sheep
2 oxen; mice; feet; women; children
3 goose; mouse; tooth; foot; woman
4 mice; sheep, geese, oxen; Children
5 There were two women, three men and four children on the bus. How many feet are there? (Don't forget the driver!) Answer: twenty
6 deer: a shy animal; dear: special or not cheap
7 deer; dear; Dear

Unit 16

1 Circle in green: star, stalk, stool; circle in blue: string, stripes, strong
2 string; stick; stripe; stray; steal
3 Sounds like **fit**: stick, strip, string; sounds like **side**: stripe; sounds like **stop**: strong; sounds like **feel**: street, steal, stream; sounds like **make**: stale, stray
4 stray; street; stick; steal; stale
5 steam; struck; stain; sting; stung
6 in – ring – string; am – tram – stream or am – team – stream
7 steal; steel

Unit 17

1 witch, ditch, stitch; fetch, stretch; catch, match, hatch
2 witch, watch
3 switch; chicken; church; witch
4 Across: 1. stitch; 4. itchy; 6. hutch; 7. fetch.
Down: 1. stretch; 2. catch; 3. kitchen; 5. hatch
5 witch; Which
6 matches; watches; patches

Unit 18

1 chickens; shoelaces; classes; watches; streets; wishes
2 coats; planes; children; witches, stripes; tomatoes; jellyfish
3 ch: right box; i: middle box; th: right box; ck: middle box; sh: right box; y: right box; st: right box; str: left box
4 wand – watch; thumb – hutch; grew – blue; road – bone; geese – stream
5 wished; stripped; liked; chewed; ate; watched
6 driving; walking; stopping; running; waking; stretching
7 thum**b**; **w**rist; lis**t**en; **k**nife
8 Words to be circled: new; raincote; nees; pulld; streat.
Correct spelling: knew; raincoat; knees; pulled; street

Unit 19

1 boil, foil, spoil; nail, sail, pail, fail, trail; strain, plain, chain, brain
2 coil, coin; rail, rain
3 ail/sail/nail; soil/oil; ail/tail/rail; joy; join; air/airy/fair/far
4 toy box; toilet
5 tray; snail trail
6 chain; join
7 Sentences will vary.

Unit 20

1 Circle all.
2 jelly; donkey; shield; thief; turkey; monkey
3 turkey; donkey: monkey
4 chief; carry; worry; donkey
5 carry; empty; chief; monkey
6 thief; key; empty; field; chief; carry; worry

Unit 21

1 babies; ladies; puppies; jellies; fairies; ponies
2 carries; hurries; cries; flies; worries
3 pony; worry; lolly; dry; daisy; dry; daisy; carry; turkey; enjoy
4 fairies; babies; lollies, puppies; ladies; ponies
5 monkeys; fairies; bullies; stories

Unit 22

1 paw, claw, draw, law
2 Pics to be circled: wall; door
3 lawn, dawn, yawn; crawl, shawl
4 Words to be circled: door; shore; roar; poor; four; more; for; floor
5 **oor**: poor/floor; **or**: for/nor; **our**: four; **ore**: pore/fore/bore/store/chore/core/more/wore; **oar**: roar/soar
6 sore – hurting, saw – looked at; raw – not cooked, roar – loud sound; paw – an animal's foot, poor – not rich, pour – tip out of a jug; draw – sketch a picture, drawer – place to put things
7 poor, paw; sore, drawer; roar, raw

Unit 23

1 splash; thread; throw; spray; spring; scratch; scream; split
2 Words to be circled: spray; strike; thread; how
3 scratch; spring; spray; split; shrink
4 cream/ream/seam/sea/cram/ram/am; how/row/tow; tread/read/head; ill/sill/hill; ash/lash/spa/as
5 spring; summer; winter; autumn (Other words will vary.)
Autumn has a silent *n*.
6 sprint; thrill; splinter

Unit 24

1 teeth; rain; read; pour; shield; boil, prawn; door
2 sore/soar; whole; pour/poor/pore; knew; raw
3 worries; splashes; writing; threw; tripped; draws; scraped; sailing
4 crawl; empty; spring; thief; thread; field
5 monkey; chief; scratch; straw; spoil; shrink; draw
Clues will vary.
6 Answers will vary.

Unit 25

1 I'm: I am; he's: he is; isn't: is not; can't: cannot; won't: will not
2 she's; doesn't; we're
3 can't; It's; don't; we're
4 his; he's
5 There; Their; They're
6 Sentences will vary.

Unit 26

1 proudly, sadly, strongly, quickly, softly
2 nicely; rudely; safely
3 happily; shyly
4 Long vowel: sadly; loudly; nicely; rudely; kindly
Short vowel: quickly; crossly; happily
Short and long vowels: quietly
5 Answers will vary.
6 The postman spoke to me crossly.
I patted the dog kindly.

Unit 27

1 Pics to be circled: bird; shirt; fern; girl
2 girl; fern; bird; first; dirty; birthday
3 shirt, bird, birth, girl, girth, first, dirt, third, thirst
4 dirtier; bigger; later; quieter; thinner; heavier
5 dirty; thirsty; her
6 Recounts will vary.

Unit 28

1 burn, turn, churn; purse, nurse, curse
2 word, work, worm, worth, worse
3 curly; nurse; worm; turn; words
4 burn; curly; work; hurt; burst
5 worm, purse; burst, hurt, nurse, work, burn
6 Words with **ur**: fur, turn, nurse. Word with **er**: her. Words with **ir**: shirt, thirst, third, dirt, dirty. Word with **or**: worth

Unit 29

1 1st pic: teacher; 2nd pic: sailor; 3rd pic: actor; 4th pic: doctor
2 doctor; baker; sailor; author; actor
3 builder; inspector; editor; painter; cleaner; manager
4 Trevor is clever at solving puzzles.
Mum's favourite flowers are yellow roses.
Sailors often practise on the river.
5 Sentences will vary.

Unit 30

1 worm; first; hurt; fern
2 I'll; can't; it's; won't; isn't; you're
3 sunflower; newspaper; wheelchair
4 actor; farmer; visitor; driver; builder; zookeeper; hairdresser; author; teacher
5 nurse; sailor
6 quickly; cleverly; nicely; strongly; happily; thirstily
7 unlucky; undress; untidy; unhappy
8 Words to be circled: flowrs; werms; offen; quikly; visiters.
Correct spelling: flowers; worms; often; quickly; visitors

Unit 31

1 Friday; Tuesday; Monday; Saturday; Wednesday
2 **S**: Saturday, Sunday; **T**: Tuesday, Thursday
3 Answers will vary.
4 Answers will vary.
5 Monday; Tuesday; Wednesday; Thursday; Friday; Saturday
Sentences will vary.
6 Answers will vary.

Unit 32

1 high, sigh, thigh; night, sight, light, right, might, bright, flight, tight
2 highest/tallest; brightest; closest
3 Words to be circled: nite; tryed; burnd; britely; highe.
Correct spelling: night; tried; burned; brightly; high
4 eye; nose; chin; ear; mouth; neck; elbow; chest; hand; thigh; knee; foot
5 Answers will vary.
6 sigh, high, height, tight, flight, light

Unit 33

1 build; would/could/should/wouldn't; world; scold/shoulder/ mouldy/boulder
2 could, would, should, mould
Different vowel sound: mould
3 should; could; would
4 couldn't; wouldn't; shouldn't; I'd
5 wild; mould; mouldy; gold; bald; sold; shoulder; scold
6 boulder; bolder
7 Sentences will vary.

Unit 34

1 nothing
2 some/body; every/one; no/body; any/where; every/where; no/thing; any/thing; no/where; some/where; every/thing; any/one; some/times; every/body; some/how
3 someone, something, sometime, sometimes, somehow, somewhere; nowhere, anywhere, somewhere, everywhere, wherever
4 nothing; someone; everywhere; another
5 anybody, anyhow, anyone, anything, anyway, anywhere

Unit 35

1 teacher; claw; jacket; thumb; flower
2 fern; glue; road; chain; doctor
3 jokes; hairbrushes; classes; babies; branches; potatoes; children; sheep
4 give – five – fire – wire; grew – grow – glow – flow; some – home – hope – hops; boat – beat – bean – been
5 On Monday, Ben is reading. On Tuesday, Ben is playing football. On Wednesday, Ben is running. On Thursday, Ben is flying a kite. On Friday, Ben is swimming. On Saturday, it is ______________.
Answers for last sentence will vary.
6 soap; light; worm; thief
7 called; yelled; screamed; shouted; whispered
8 Answers will vary. For example: shouted/yelled; whispered/ cried/sobbed; called/shouted; asked